If You Could See What I See

Also by Sylvia Browne

If You Could See What I See

The Tenets of Novus Spiritus

Sylvia Browne

HAY HOUSE, INC.
Carlsbad, California
London • Sydney • Johannesburg
Vancouver • Hong Kong

Published and distributed in the United States by: Hay House, Inc., P.O. Box 5100, Carlsbad, CA 92018-5100 • *Phone:* (760) 431-7695 or (800) 654-5126 • *Fax:* (760) 431-6948 or (800) 650-5115 • www.hayhouse.com • *Published and distributed in Australia by:* Hay House Australia Pty. Ltd., 18/36 Ralph St., Alexandria NSW 2015 • *Phone:* 612-9669-4299 • *Fax:* 612-9669-4144 • www.hayhouse.com.au • *Published and distributed in the United Kingdom by:* Hay House UK, Ltd. • Unit 62, Canalot Studios • 222 Kensal Rd., London W10 5BN • *Phone:* 44-20-8962-1230 • *Fax:* 44-20-8962-1239 • www.hayhouse.co.uk • *Published and distributed in the Republic of South Africa by:* Hay House SA (Pty), Ltd., P.O. Box 990, Witkoppen 2068 • *Phone/Fax:* 27-11-706-6612 • orders@psdprom.co.za • *Distributed in Canada by:* Raincoast • 9050 Shaughnessy St., Vancouver, B.C. V6P 6E5 • *Phone:* (604) 323-7100 • *Fax:* (604) 323-2600

Editorial supervision: Jill Kramer • *Design:* Tricia Breidenthal

Library of Congress Cataloging-in-Publication Data

Browne, Sylvia.
  If you could see what I see : the tenets of Novus Spiritus / Sylvia Browne.
    p. cm.
  ISBN-13: 978-1-4019-0648-1 (hardcover)
  ISBN-10: 1-4019-0648-6 (hardcover)
  1. Spiritual life--Miscellanea. 2. Gnosticism--Miscellanea. 3. Society of Novus Spiritus (Campbell, Calif.) I. Title.
  BF1999.B755 2006
  299'.93--dc22
                              2005022803

Hardcover **ISBN 13:** 978-1-4019-0648-1
Hardcover **ISBN 10:** 1-4019-0648-6

Tradepaper **ISBN 13:** 978-1-4019-0784-6
Tradepaper **ISBN 10:** 1-4019-0784-9

09 08 07 06   4 3 2 1
1st printing, January 2006

Printed in the United States of America

*I want to thank Angelia,
my granddaughter, for
helping me with research,
and Darren English for
his great help in tracking
Gnostic philosophy with me*

I

*The way of all peace is to scale the mountain of self.
Loving others makes the climb down easier. We see all
things darkly until love lights the lamp of our soul.*

II

Whatever thou lovest, lovest thou.

III

*Do not give unto God any human pettiness such as
vengeance, wrath, or hate. Negativity is man's alone.*

IV

*Create your own heaven, not a hell.
You are a creator made from God.*

V

*Turn thy power outward, not inward,
for therein shines the light and the way.*

VI

*In faith be like the wind chimes: Hold steady
until faith, like the wind, moves you to joy.*

VII

*Know that each life is a path winding toward perfection.
It is the step after step that is hard, not the whole of the journey.*

VIII

*Be simple. Allow no man to judge you,
not even yourself, for you cannot judge God.*

IX

You are a light in a lonely, dark desert who enlightens many.

X

*Let no one convince you that you are less than a God.
Do not let fear imprison your spiritual growth.*

XI

*Do not allow the unfounded belief in demons
to block your communion with God.*

XII

The body is a living temple unto God,
wherein we worship the spark of the Divine.

XIII

God does not create the adversities in life.
By your own choice they exist to aid in your perfection.

XIV

Karma is nothing more than honing the wheel of evolvement.
It is not retribution, but merely a balancing of experiences.

XV

God allows each person the opportunity for perfection, whether you
need one life or a hundred lives to reach your level of perfection.

XVI

Devote your life, your soul, your very existence, to the
service of God. For only there will you find meaning in life.

XVII

War is profane; defense is compulsory.

XVIII

Death is the act of returning Home; it should be done with grace
and dignity. You may preserve that dignity by refusing prolonged
use of artificial life-support systems. Let God's will be done.

XIX

We believe in a Mother God, Who is
co-Creator with our all-loving Father God.

XX

We believe that our Lord was crucified, but did not die
on the cross. Instead, he went on to live his life in France
with his mother and Mary Magdalene, his wife.

XXI

We Gnostics kept the knowledge hidden that Christ's lineage
exists even today, and the truth long buried is open to research.

CONTENTS

Dear God,

As the years pass like the dead leaves in autumn, let me never lose sight of You. Let me always walk with my hand in Yours, and when human beings may fail me and all hope seems to die, let me feel You walking beside me.

I have a great journey ahead of me, by which I am master of. If it lasts for only a day or stretches throughout many years, keep me pure of heart and true to the principles I hold so high. Let me always be patient with those around me. Let me see life at its fullest and yet smile bravely at death. Let me see and appreciate the beauty of Your creations and the extent of Your power. Only when I have done these things will I be able to look to heaven and know "I have lived."

Through the years when my dreams fall around me, I will know that dreams should not only be made up of hope that stretches like a translucent web over reality, but built out of the hope that burns into the future and is left in our lighthouse of memories.

Sylvia Shoemaker (Browne)
Notation in my Bible . . . May 1954

INTRODUCTION

It's been almost 20 years since I wrote my first book, *Adventures of a Psychic*. As I look back, it seems like yesterday . . . and yet a lifetime away (like so many things). To recap just a bit, as most of you know I was born psychic, as my grandmother Ada Coil was, and her mother and her mother before her—and on it goes for approximately 300 years. My son Christopher Dufresne also has the gift and has taken up the family mantle; today he is an established psychic in his own right.

Throughout my life, especially since *Adventures of a Psychic* came out, my soul has been tried to the limit. Everyone thinks that because you're on television or are in the public eye, you're living a glamorous, wealthy life. Not true—I walk the same path you do. While my psychic ability isn't affected by "normalcy" (which I give God credit for), Sylvia Browne the woman still goes through hurt, joy, pain, worry over family and friends, divorce, bills, cars breaking down, a garage flooding, and on and on it goes. . . .

I've spent many a sleepless night worrying about people I can't get to fast enough. I pray that I'm doing God's work every day. I get nervous before I go onstage to do a lecture or workshop . . . again praying that I'm able to help others and do God's work. I try to put up with the mean-spirited detractors (not skeptics—those are normal), but just to be a target for someone's hateful, unfounded untruths hurts. I find as I get older, however, that I pay less attention to it. I never really got involved in negative publicity, but I worry about the younger psychics coming up who aren't as thick-skinned as I am. I keep telling them that if we're doing the best we can for God, no one can take anything away from us.

What keeps me going are the 21 tenets you'll find in this book.

When I've gone back to the words contained herein, I've gained such strength. At times they've seemed like a map for life, while other times they're almost a prayer or a meditation. In this work, not only will I explore each one in depth, but I'll also incorporate stories from my own life that illustrate them. When we look at the tenets from different angles, we can see that they take in *all* of life, including what bedevils us or makes us happy on our spiritual quest.

Discovering the Tenets

These 21 principles came directly from my spirit guide Francine. For those of you who don't know, Francine has been with me my entire life. I first "heard" her at the age of seven, for I'm not only a trance medium and clairvoyant, but I'm also *clairaudient,* which means that I hear my spirit guide talk to me. Although I hear her, I can't take listening to her for very long because her voice comes into my right ear and sounds like a bad Alvin and the Chipmunks record. I therefore prefer to go into trance and have Francine speak through me and give me information. The tenets came from her while I was in such a state, and they were brought back from the ancient Gnostic texts. Even before the Dead Sea Scrolls and the Nag Hammadi were made public, Francine had already related what mirrors many of the passages of Thomas and James, which are part of the Nag Hammadi scrolls.

These tenets have been a part of the Sylvia Browne Corporation for about 30 years—even before the Society of Novus Spiritus was ever established as an accredited church and religious organization by the state of California. They were our rules to live by. Now, while these 21 principles might seem very simplistic, when you go deeper into them you'll discover that they're far more spiritual, and in many ways carry a deeper meaning, than they may seem to be on the surface. Maybe if you could see what I see or hear what I hear doing 15 to 20 readings a day, you'd know that their depth goes far beyond what the words seem to hold. It's almost like the Mona Lisa's enigmatic smile: What does it mean? What secret is she keeping from us? What does she know that we don't?

Here I'm going to do something I've never done before: I'll go through the tenets one by one and show you how they relate to me and my journey. Some of you may respond to what I discuss, while others may feel that it's too far out there for you. Just think of what I'm about to share with you as a chronicle of a life—that is, don't simply look at it as a *psychic* life. Of course that's part of it, but so much of these principles refer to all of our lives in one form or another.

In the tenets of our Society, and the stories that accompany them, you'll see your existence (and that of your loved ones) reflected; you'll also note how we struggle to get happiness out of life and not succumb to that dark place of futility or depression. This book is not a course, but rather a very direct commentary on things we don't understand. Maybe I can shine a light on it so that it's not so confusing.

Gnostics and Novus Spiritus

You'll see that this book is an autobiography in a sense, but it almost has to be to show you how I came upon these tenets, which are the cornerstone of our church's beliefs. I started (or, should I say, "attempted to start") a Society in 1973, but it became a nonprofit foundation for research of the paranormal. As life so often turns in wondrous ways, we did investigate everything from astral projection to past lives, psychic phenomena, hauntings, poltergeist activities—

you name it—and all the while, a strong survival of the soul and spirituality was coming out . . . not just in droplets, but floods of knowledge of the afterlife, including our purpose and our learning for God. My staff and I kept copious notes and statistics—in fact, our archives are filled with affidavits too numerous to mention and too similar to disregard.

Take, for instance, the afterlife. How could so many people, when finding themselves on the Other Side through various means (including near-death experiences, astral trips, dreams, and past-life regressions), find the same topography, buildings, research, services, and even populace searching for the God we know and love? These were everyday people from different countries, creeds, religions, and backgrounds who had been immersed in widely varying schools of thought.

One of the things I'm grateful for is that today, the Society of Novus Spiritus is thriving, with hundreds of study groups around the world. For years the Gnostic movement has tried to form a religious organization, whether it was the Cathars, the Knights Templar, or the Essenes, and all were either wiped out by the Catholic Church and reigning powers, or they went underground. A Gnostic is one who searches for truth constantly with the grace of an all-loving and all-knowing God, and uses spirituality and love as their weapons against negativity. A Gnostic also holds truth in the highest esteem, for only with truth can you find true spirituality and be as one with God.

The remnants of the movement today basically consist of the Freemasons and Rosicrucians, which are more fraternal and philanthropic organizations than religious ones. I'm positive that there are some Gnostic organizations out there, but they're basically either kept private and secret or they've gone totally underground. You'll find a few of them on the Internet, but they don't have any religious services to speak of and are mostly information sites.

The Gnostic movement is very ancient and wasn't just confined to Christianity, as most people think. In actual fact, it existed before the time of Christ, but was mostly obliterated by the 5th century after the Roman emperor Theodorus I officially recognized only one branch of Catholicism. Now I'm not trying to single out the Catholics as the only persecutors of the Gnostics, but their history isn't exactly bloodless or lily white. The Romans and the Sanhedrin also did their share of persecution in trying to put down what they called "rabble-rousing groups" that ran around like Jesus did and taught and followed the philosophy of an all-loving God. Gnostics have been burned, tortured, and driven out, whether it was in France or Jerusalem or other parts of the world. They were either killed and their possessions taken, or they went underground and met secretly for fear of reprisal from the religious politics of the Church or the establishment at that time.

The Gnostics have risen up at least four times and were put to death, branded as heretics, and just got tired of the embattlement of the fear-based churches, so they disbanded publicly . . . only to quietly keep their beliefs buried in their hearts and secret societies. They had their various schools of thought and theology (as most religions do) brought forth by different scholars, prophets, or leaders. Perhaps the most famous was Valentinus, who founded a Gnostic movement in the 2nd century A.D. that spread throughout the Middle East, North Africa, and Europe. The Valentinian school existed for more than 600 years and still has influence today despite constant persecution from the Church.

As the Gnostic movement was waning due to persecution, another movement arose that was founded by the inspirational writings of the prophet Mani. The Manichaean movement spread not only to Europe, but to Central Asia and China as well, and it still exists in small pockets today. Both of these movements incorporated reincarnation in their philosophy and advocated it strongly, and both had numerous writings attributed to them of an apocryphal nature. Several of these Gnostic movements can be studied at **www.gnosis.org**, with many related links to other

Websites that also provide much insight into Gnosticism.

Gnostics are not a threat to anyone except those who want occult control. We accept everyone; and profess religious tolerance and an all-loving God Who gets rid of the fear, guilt, and karma that has been laid on the shoulders of humankind (which both kept people in line *and* gained more members for various religions).

* * *

I do want to pause here to clear up some information about Gnosticism and our church. Not only has Gnosticism been around for thousands of years, with philosophers such as Plato espousing it, but there are many schools or teachers out there in the world today. Not all of Gnosticism is Christian based, and even Christian Gnosticism has different sects and beliefs. There are many aspects of Gnosticism that Novus Spiritus doesn't practice or believe in, but we *have* tried to form a religion that has its basis in Gnosticism and one that especially follows the teachings of Christ and the dualism of our Creators (that is, Mother and Father God).

At the Society of Novus Spiritus, we don't purport to know every truth. Since the whole concept of Gnosis essentially means to "seek truth," we're constantly in flux as we do so. That's why we basically have no church-made dogma or rules other than the "golden rule"—that is, we try to help others by doing good works with love—and the belief in our Lord (Jesus) and the duality of God. Our 21 tenets reflect what we believe, and they're added to as truth becomes apparent.

We accept all, regardless of their beliefs, race, ethnic background, gender, and so forth. No one is turned away, especially those who are seeking truth, enlightenment, or a loving God. We have services, but we just talk about God's love and light and the Christ Consciousness; we also do meditations and pray for the sick. After a service, we do healings wherein we have people stand up and tell the congregation what they need, and we pray for them. We have a prayer line that goes 24/7. We have literally hundreds of study groups where we meet in someone's home and discuss the tenets, as people did many years ago—we've tried to reproduce how it was in the time of Christ. We also do research, give solace to each other, and help the sick and the elderly. It's a moving, hands-on, living spirituality that's promoted by all.

So the Society of Novus Spiritus, which is going into its 19th year, has spread across the United States and other countries in hundreds of study groups. We used to meet in our offices in Campbell, California, but our congregation grew to be too big. Now we have four so-called churches (or I should say "meeting places"), and we're still growing.

Who Am I to Start a Church?

I won't ever lie to you, but to form Novus Spiritus was very frightening to me. This is where I had to put my silly ego aside. For perhaps a week I walked around muttering to Francine, "It's bad enough to put yourself out there as a psychic, but now we want to start a church!"

She replied, "Do you know how many religions were started from a vision or a revelation? Quakers, Mormons, even Moses and his burning bush."

This made me feel better, especially when I looked at Buddha and his enlightenment or Mohammed and his message. Now please understand that I'm not implying I'm comparable to these messengers, but there is truth in revelation and spiritual communication. This truth isn't mine alone, but it has logically sprung from what I've researched for more than 50 years, compounded with the considerable amount of research from so many thousands that I've read for, as well as the work of our church's ministers and others from around the world.

Anyway, the Society of Novus Spiritus was founded and accredited, and the tenets that had sat there gathering dust began to take hold and form the basis for our beliefs. They seem to echo the Beatitudes from the Sermon on the Mount, the Eightfold Path of Buddhism, and the gentle portions of text from the Koran—and they serve to bring into focus the simplicity of what every one of them tried to say. The tenets aren't new (they're as old as time), but they have been condensed. The ministers and I often say, "After we've gone to the Other Side, we hope that humankind doesn't corrupt the simplicity that's so real and tangible, which carries such a gut-level truth."

It's interesting to note that since my books have come out, the e-mails and letters have poured in, and each in their own way has said, "This says what I've felt forever," "I always believed, but was afraid to say it for fear that people would think I was different or crazy," or "I know this is right, not only in what my heart tells me, but my intellect confirms it."

So the 21 tenets were formed out of our Gnostic philosophy, and the only problem we encountered was that when people thought about God, they tended to think in the singular sense of God the Father. Thus, we added a tenet to recognize the duality of God and to acknowledge the existence of God the *Mother*. Several of our tenets are also highly controversial to standard Christian belief, but by no means do they take away from the Divinity or teachings of Christ. Yes, they impugn the beliefs of the early Christian church in some areas that are still believed in today, but new information and research in the last few years is starting to show that these beliefs are false anyway.

I'm highly controversial as it stands, so why not just put all the truth out there for everyone to read and see . . . besides, where would the fun be if I didn't? So, having said that, I hope that you enjoy accompanying me on the very personal journey I'll be taking you on in these pages.

✳ ✳ ✳ ✳ ✳ ✳

TENET I

The way of all peace is to scale the mountain of self. Loving others makes the climb down easier. We see all things darkly until love lights the lamp of our soul.

My life started out being psychic, and maybe thanks to sheer ignorance, I went with it. God knows that it hasn't been an easy road, but I'd never change it. It's been rewarding, of course, but I've also experienced rejection and skepticism of the highest order. Yet when we write our chart (the life plan we plot out before we're even born) and have a goal for God and our own soul's perfection, we follow it the best way we can.

When I wrote *Adventures of a Psychic,* many individuals I mentioned in it were still alive, so I had to couch what my life had been like in somewhat vague terms. People are very smart, so when I wrote about my childhood, they read between the lines. . . . Now, however, so many of them are gone that I can go into greater depth about what my life was really like.

Shortly after my first book was written, I had to declare bankruptcy and was hit with an astronomical IRS bill. This was because my then-husband Dal, out of ignorance, not malice, opened up a gold mine recommended by an attorney. He forgot to fill out a securities form, so they came down on us like a ton of bricks. I'll never forget the judge saying, "It's unfortunate, Mrs. Browne, but you're the one making the money, so you'll have to pay. I'm very sorry."

Now in my experience (as probably in yours), when you fall in love there doesn't seem to be any mountain too high to climb. We can almost float up rather than climb because we're so euphoric and our endorphins are racing, not to mention our hormones. But when that goes south, the journey down is miserably hard—we feel foolish, battered, rejected, and bruised in our soul. We then look valiantly for someone to love, or who loves us, after the long journey of paranoia, suspicion, and hurt begins to dim. For some it (sadly) never does, and they spend their lives in the nightmare of what could have been. They don't understand that not everyone needs to be paired—and what if it doesn't work out if they *do* find someone else?

When I was a young girl, I truly dreamed of a house and children and a husband who loved and supported me. Well, when my chances came, I kept telling myself, *It's not right*. For example, I was engaged to two men who loved and wanted to make a home with me. Both of them later did get married, had children, and supported their wives. One of these wonderful guys died just a few months ago, and one of the last conversations we had (yes, we kept track of each other over all those years) points out the differences of our charts and the "what could have been" scenarios.

I started out by asking him, "What if it had been the other way and I had agreed to marry you?"

Joe wisely replied, "No, Sylvia, it wouldn't have worked. The world was calling you so loudly that even I could hear it." But still, in the human part of our brain we wonder (chart or no chart), *What if?*

And that's how I felt when my marriage to Dal broke up. We divorced partly because of my anger resulting from trying to be so loyal and above board, even as I let someone else foolishly jeopardize the church and foundation I'd built. I went from having not one smudge on my record to people running amuck with money I didn't have. But it was my fault, too, because I was so busy with lectures, ministers, and readings that I left the business end to someone who'd made a catastrophic and foolish mistake.

I felt that my life was over. My home and car were gone, and all my possessions had to be sold. I had no credit, so I had to try to pay for everything in cash. On top of that, I was taking care of my aging parents and my friends Linda and Larry. (Linda is a kindred spirit who's been with me almost 30 years, while Larry was a friend who was trying to help me out of the mess I was in.) My father had some money and helped me some, but since he'd worked all his life for what he had, I couldn't take his nest egg. Consequently, I had to raise enough money to get us all a place to live. The two apartments we wanted would cost $1,100 each, for a total of $2,200. I remember the day we had a huge garage sale . . . during which we made $2,300. I got my mom and dad an apartment; and Linda, Larry, and I got one adjacent to it.

Talk about your uphill climbs! The economy at that time in the late '80s was pretty bad, but I managed. I started to do 25 readings a day to keep my church, family, and staff going. I never missed a payroll. My son Chris, who was barely starting his psychic career, helped some, but it was just enough to keep him afloat because he'd recently gotten married. They say these things are cathartic, but the memories are still painful and debilitating. But wait . . . it gets better and then worse—which is the story of all our lives.

My parents were in their late 80s at the time, and they were failing. My mother's behavior, which was always a real nightmare, was becoming more erratic. My father (who was working with me) was also taking a turn for the worse. On top of that, my book *My Guide, Myself* (later to be known as *Adventures of a Psychic* and published by Hay House) had flopped because the publisher, New American Library, had been sold to Dutton, leaving my book to fall through the cracks. And *People Are Talking,* a local show in the San Francisco area—on which I often appeared and had been my main public-relations (PR) outlet—was suddenly canceled.

Larry, my friend since he was 19, tried to keep my spirits up, but it was hard. I have a tendency when things go wrong to pull in and away and regroup inside myself and go forward. Not because I resent help, but as you know, there are times when no one can help you but you. Every area I looked at seemed pretty hopeless, but as I've taught and do believe, you stay in the light and keep on going.

I started traveling to other states to set up "in person" readings, as my PR outlets were at a standstill. Then Steve Ober, an old producer friend of mine from *People Are Talking* who was now producing in Los Angeles, called and asked me to be on *AM Los Angeles* with host Steve Edwards. So I went . . . and watched as my numerous appearances caused my PR to pick up. Yet I was still grieving over the end of my marriage and the fact that my life was in financial ruin—plus, I was really feeling the strain of trying to keep my staff and Novus Spiritus afloat.

It was during this time (which I called "the dark period") that I happened to pick up the tenets, and at that moment, I began to see their surface *and* deeper meanings. "Dear God," I whispered, "this is truly the treasure map to keep us on track." It reminds me of a painting that used to hang in my grandmother's home, which depicted a woman standing against a rock on the ocean. Her hair was back, and she looked as if she was being battered by the weather. Her arms were thrown wide open, but again, like the Mona Lisa, there was that smile. This time, it seemed to convey, "Bring on the waves and the storms—I can stand it! I will embrace it and be strong!"

My grandmother used to say two things that I carry with me: "Within your weakness lies your strength sleeping" and

"Save your tears for when you really need them." Well, I was recently in the room of my 12-year-old granddaughter, Angelia, while she was doing her homework. I sat down on the bed and happened to glance over at a piece of paper that looked as if it had been torn from a diary. It said, "I must remember as Bagdah [that's her name for me] says, to save my tears for when I need them, but it was hard to lose my pet mouse." I didn't say a word, but my heart ached as all of us do when someone we love feels pain, yet I was also very proud that something I'd said hit home.

A friend of mine whom I'd first met and read for more than 20 years ago in Kenya (where she was a journalist) just called me. She's writing a book that starts out with a reading I'd given her many years ago, which she hadn't believed at the time. I'd told her that she was going to get divorced, move to California, and receive an award for her son. I truly didn't see his death—looking back, I should have been able to warn her, but then I also know that I wasn't supposed to. You see, the young man had to fulfill his destiny, and if I'd seen his death, it might have taken him off course. I always pick up things for a reason, and I don't always know that reason or why I don't get something—other than the fact that it might derail someone from their chart.

Anyway, my friend is now divorced and living in California. She also received a posthumous award for her son from the State Department—for he was a photographer killed in Bosnia. She managed to climb her own mountain, and now she's writing and helping other mothers who have lost children. And she's truly happy.

Everything passes and everything changes—what's bad today can turn on a dime tomorrow, and what's good can also turn bad—none of it lasts. If we're depressed (and some people do need pharmaceutical help due to chemical imbalances in the brain), we can alleviate it by loving outside of, and getting above, ourselves. All the lights will come on, especially the light of the soul.

I'm reminded of a family I just saw in Florida who wanted

a private session because of the death of a loved one. The mother asked me, "What do I do with the rest of my life?"

I said, "Well, you have your grandson, your daughter, your husband, and your friends; and maybe you can go out eventually and help other mothers who have lost children."

She visibly brightened and then hesitantly asked, "Is my son really happy?"

"He's happier than we are," I replied.

I know that type of advice isn't much consolation at times, but it sure is an absolute truth that those on the Other Side are better off than we are. After all, they've finished the journey of climbing this mountain—not only of self, but of adversity and negativity. Their lamp is lit, and they've gone to the Home we'll all go to one day.

How Can This Tenet Help You?

From a spiritual standpoint, the whole meaning of this first tenet points to climbing the mountain of your own ego, or the false self that can fool you and lure you into believing that you're more than you are. The mountain of ego isn't that difficult to climb if you begin to realize it only means the *essence* of you, or the sum total of who you are, including all the good and bad. Climbing this mountain is difficult until you come to the understanding that you're a spiritual being who came here to experience for God and yourself. When you get that, then it's just like being in physical love: You'll float down the mountain and realize that loving others really does light the lamp of our soul.

Now how did *I* climb the mountain of self? I don't have much false ego—not because I'm necessarily such a good person—I've just always been so external. But I did have a tough time with my ability. When it came to seeing and hearing things, I just wanted to turn it off at times. It isn't that I don't love my psychicness, but I certainly didn't want to be viewed as "crazy." (Strangely enough, when I was a schoolteacher, the priests, nuns, and even the kids just took it in stride that I was different, or it was just "Sylvia's thing.")

Francine and my psychic grandmother tried to explain that I came from a long line of psychics, but I'd gone to college and taken abnormal psychology. For all I knew, we could be a long line of genetically flawed people with an aberration of the mind. I very stubbornly stuck to this viewpoint until the day Francine asked me, "Have you ever had any motive to hurt anyone?"

"Of course not!" I answered angrily.

"Are you more right than wrong?" she countered.

"Well, yes," I replied. "I guess so."

"Have you made people feel better with the truth?"

"I suppose . . . ," I said.

Then she asked, "Sylvia, why don't you live with it and do it for God, and quit trying to scientifically put it in a box?" So not really having much choice, I did climb the mountain of myself and gave it all up to God. I also had encouragement from some people who just seemed to find me.

Even today before each lecture, TV appearance, book signing, or reading, I take a deep breath and ask God to keep me a pure channel. I also surround everyone with the White Light of the Holy Spirit and ask that my insight be clear and clean and that no part of Sylvia get in the way.

I can't say this enough: *If you get out of yourself and give to God, you get out of your own way.* Is it hard? Sure it is, but your love and passion for something outside of you makes your spiritual engines run. Sure, the corny expression "If life gives you lemons, make lemonade" is great, but it better be sweet or else you're just left with sour lemon water. The sugar is what you add to life.

When you stop to help a person, and truly love them unconditionally for who they are, you're fulfilling your chart. In turn, you'll like or even love yourself for the good that you've done. I think it's very important to do this many times, without fanfare and recognition. It's like that movie *Pay It Forward,* or what my ministers and I call "a magnificent obsession"—that is, to prove what people have wandered the world to be assured of: that God is good and loves us unconditionally.

My staff often jokes in a kind way that I can have a temperature of 103° (which I've had) and be as sick as a dog, yet I still go on reading. I've gone on after deaths in my family, a hurtful divorce, and so on, and my ability seems to work aside (or *be*side or *in*side) of me without anything interfering with it. I was doing readings six days after a hysterectomy that I had when I was 40. Is it constitution? Maybe, but the ability is far beyond my physical self.

So on whatever level you choose to look at the first tenet, it begins to take on new meaning—as it has for me every time I read it. Francine has also said to "be above the body" because we're only "renting" this vehicle for a time. Our soul is larger than our body, and if we get too earthbound, we're going to get too caught up in the woes of this world.

Shakespeare said that a coward dies many times before his death. No one on this planet can ever be a coward, since just to come down here is an act of bravery. The only cowardice that comes into play is when you sink into darkness and forget how to love. It doesn't matter if it's for your animals, your friends, your garden, or your family, the key here is *"to love."* So light your lamp of love, and the world that may seem dark becomes the light of your own Christ consciousness (or whatever your beliefs may be).

✳ ✳ ✳ ✳ ✳ ✳

TENET II

Whatever thou lovest, lovest thou.

I'm sure that your reaction when you first read this tenet was like my own: "Hey, that isn't always true." When we love others, we have the high expectation that they're going to love us back, but I've certainly cared deeply for another person and not had that feeling returned. Well, I'm not just talking about the affection between a man and woman here, although that takes up a big part of the "loving game." Poetry and literature certainly have that passion as their dominating feature, but we also love parents, children, friends, relatives, pets, and so on.

So many times we do pick the wrong person to care about because, as I'm convinced, love is not only blind, but deaf and dumb as well. Yet we can't just blame everyone else. We have to be honest with ourselves: Are we lovable, or are we too demanding? Are our expectations beyond the norm of reality? Are we in the state of loving someone unconditionally? The majority of us mothers (good ones, that is) love our children in this way. We might not always like what our kids do, but we love them without reservation. Even "tough love" has an unconditional component in that the mother really does hope that her child will straighten up for his or her own good.

In the many readings that I do, I hear variations on the same theme from my clients: "My husband of 25 [or 30 or 35] years left me." And a doctor friend recently told me that almost half of his patients are women being treated for depression over their husbands leaving. But let's not leave men out—sorry ladies, but in my experience, it's not just the men who cheat . . . women do, too, and frequently. The only defining line here is that women don't tend to tell, and they usually don't break up their families over an indiscretion.

In no circumstance do I believe that a person should stay with an abusive spouse. I did in my first marriage, because I was ashamed and thought it was my fault. But keep in mind that abuse can be mental as well as physical, and women (who from the beginning of time have been the keepers of hearth and home) often put up with it longer than we should. Society has always had a tendency to blame the woman, from Eve to the modern-day divorce that happens because the wife didn't make the husband happy. Just as so many therapists blame the mother when a child goes wrong—no one stops to think that maybe this just is a rotten kid!

Sometimes, though, even when what we love isn't good for us, it can lead us to a better place. My first marriage, as abusive as it was, led me to California, where my career took off. There I formed a foundation where many people could work and help others (it was first the Nirvana Foundation, and then it became the Sylvia Browne Corporation).

No one on either side of my family had ever divorced, except for me. And then, with my dreams in hand, I tried it again. Dal and I did have a happy marriage for many years, but eventually it didn't work. My third (and last) husband seemed to be a kindred soul, but he left me for another woman, claiming that I was so popular now that I didn't need him! Of course I sat back and wondered, "What in God's name is *this* about?" Once again, looking on the bright side, this was not a fun time in my life, but since then my career has taken a giant step forward, and my eldest son, Paul, has stepped in to help me.

The thing I'd hoped secretly in my heart was that my sons would be part of my spiritual mission, and it happened. Chris, my precious psychic son, has worked beside me for 19 years as an excellent medium (and that isn't just a mother's pride talking . . . well, maybe some), but now my dear Paul also really helps me in my work. This would have never been possible if my last husband had stayed, because he'd tried to alienate everyone from me.

So I've had to learn just like anyone else. Every story has two sides, so perhaps I *was* too busy and caught up with my church, people, and career, causing my last marriage to go by the wayside. I have a real problem with people who take adultery lightly, but that's probably my upbringing. I have a problem with it even in my readings, and I know that it doesn't come from me—it really is linked to our Gnostic motto (which is in our logo and even in our jewelry): "Loyalty, Gratitude, and Commitment." I guess you can say that for me, adultery is more about loyalty than anything else—when I link myself up to someone, I tend to be there through hell and high water. I used to call it my "defect," but now I can thank God for that defect!

Now three years out, life is full of love again. My time is filled with friends, companionship, pets, clients, and all of you—and it's all good. A friend of mine says that having a bad relationship is like having an elephant in the front room: You can't hide it, you can't dust it off enough, and you have to clean up after it. No matter how much you pretend, it's not there.

We can also do this with the ghosts of long-lost loves,

whom we begin to make better than they were. The mind is very strange in that it has a habit of somehow forgetting the bad and remembering the good. In other words, if there were only five good times in a relationship of 20 years, that's where your mind goes, blanketing out the fights, the hurts, and the infidelities. When you think about these long-lost loves and the "what ifs," you don't have to force your mind to go to the negatives. It's time to look at things realistically: For whatever reason (yours or theirs), they didn't work out—and they never would have, no matter how much you tried to move that elephant out of your front room.

So, to go back to the second tenet, I know that it may sound like an oxymoron considering what we've been discussing, but here comes the spiritual insight. You gave your love to the wrong person . . . so where does that love go? Well, as Francine says, it's like electricity: It can never be destroyed—no, it may not have hit the target of your focus or attention, but it did go somewhere. Love is one of the emotions, believe it or not, that's stronger than hate or vengeance. It has conquered countries, built the Taj Mahal, and so on. It's the one emotion that's more pliable than all the others put together, and it can be directed easier and is more convertible than any other.

When my beloved father died, and Chris and I walked out of the hospital into that bright April day, for just a moment I wondered how people could be driving, eating lunch on the lawn, and laughing when my dad was dead. Chris looked down at me, with his beautiful blue eyes filled with tears, and asked, "What do we do now, Mom?"

I said the only thing I knew to say—or perhaps the only thing that gave reason to what I was charted for: "We go back to work and love and have compassion for all the people we talk to today in our readings."

You see, love doesn't go away . . . it stays in our hearts for our lost ones, but it also spreads out to others who love us back. I hear my clients sometimes saying, "I don't care, I just want Sam [or Suzie or whomever] to love me—I don't care about anything else!" Well, I've been there myself enough times, until spiritually I began to realize that love takes many forms.

I've been onstage many times when a voice will ring out through the darkness of the audience: "I love you, Sylvia!" I always reply, "I love you, too!" and I truly do. That phrase is so often held back, and it's a shame. That voice in the dark is someone I know either here or on the Other Side, because as I say in my lectures, we're all strung like golden beads worn around the neck of God, our all-loving Father.

My dear friend Danny Levin and I were once talking about the fact that I was so glad I'd canceled a trip to Egypt, especially when I found out that it had been hit by a bomb at one of the Hilton hotels. I laughingly said, "That's all I'd need—to be taken hostage."

Very seriously, without even a second's hesitation, he replied, "Well, I'd go in on a moment's notice with a SWAT team to get you out." Is that love? Of course it is, and it's tucked away in my memory box that reads I'VE LOVED AND BEEN LOVED.

Yet when it comes to one of the greatest love stories I've ever witnessed, I'd like to take you back with me to when I was about 12 years old. At the time, I was attending St. James Church, which was being renovated. (Those of you who are—or were—Catholics will remember how much time we spent in church: whether it was confession, choir practice, holiday and feast days, mass every day, or what have you.) Well, I remember this young construction worker who seemed to be a loner. Everyone made fun of him because he didn't seem to be attached to anyone, and every day during his lunch break, he'd dart into the church alone.

One day I heard someone half-mockingly ask, "Jack, what do you do in there?"

Jack put his head down and said, "I just run in and say, 'Jesus, this is Jack—I love you, and remember me.'"

Months went by, and we were filing in for choir practice when a scaffolding came loose and fell on Jack, killing him

13

instantly. Besides me, maybe 15 or 20 kids plus workers heard the following right above Jack's body in mid-air: "Jack, this is Jesus. I love you, too, and remember you always." Now you can say or think what you want, but we all heard it.

Would Christ or God love us no matter what? Of course, but it was the miracle of a lonely young man apparently loved by no one who truly captured the greatest love of all. Even today I get chills, and I remember it as if it were yesterday.

* * *

We can't get into the second tenet—and it certainly wouldn't be complete—if we didn't address the Christian dogma of forgiveness. Yes, we must have unconditional love, but I don't believe that we have to forgive evil. It sounds like a contradiction, I know, but think about it: If we love evil, it can't love us back, nor does it hit its mark. It's true that if love doesn't hit its mark it goes somewhere else, but why give our love to someone who's dark and unworthy? We're not at fault and we can learn from it, but we don't have to keep loving and giving and casting those proverbial pearls before such swine.

Of course we can be duped, as the Germans were by Hitler, and the people who followed Jim Jones were waylaid by occultism (which was actually evil) taking the form of love. It's not wrong to hate evil: Who's going to love the men who put millions to death for being supposed witches; and who would love Hitler, Stalin, or Manson? How sick would we have to be to love and forgive such evil creatures? The best thing to do is to give such feelings to God, but don't have guilt about experiencing these human emotions.

And keep in mind that there are some things that are just too big for us to forgive, such as a mother who has had her child needlessly killed, or a trusted family member who deceives his loved ones and takes her inheritance. I talked to a man the other day who said, "Sylvia, I raised my brother when we were growing up. Just before our dad died, my brother doctored the will and had my very ill father sign it so that he'd get everything." It wasn't just the money, which was a lot, but this man's father had promised him a ring and some keepsake photos that his brother denied him. My client went on to say, "I feel so bad—I can't forgive him!"

"Then don't," I said. "Yet don't let it take over your life."

Forgiveness is Divine, and even though we're genetically a part of God, we're not totally in the state of Divinity until we get to the Other Side. We're still in human form, just like Jesus was. Even though he was a direct reporter and messenger from God, the human side of him knew anger (in the Temple with the money changers) and despair ("Why hast thou forsaken me?"). This was his human side, just as we have the foibles of the humanness of being in a body that the soul doesn't really fit that well into.

How Can This Tenet Help You?

Instead of living with the rejection of those few people who can't or won't love you back, find someone who will. My grandmother, who was full of proverbial folksy sayings, used to say, "Sylvia, if you take your wares to a poor market, no one will buy." So true . . . if you happen to be a victim like I've been, then you can understand that gut-wrenching feeling of rejection. You feel as if your heart is broken and it will never be mended, but sorry is the person who has lost love and cannot love again.

If you fall into the trap of "Why me?" or "I did everything right and I don't deserve this" for too long, then you might as well crawl into that dark hole and stay there. All of us have a tendency to do this somewhat, but you've got to get out of it as quickly as possible, or you're going to wither away. You must excuse my use of clichés here, but sometimes they can really make a point. For example, our Lord said, "Don't cast your pearls before swine," but like me, you may have found someone and—sure enough!—you looked in your bag of love and found just a few more pearls. Well, "you can't make a silk purse out of a sow's ear" (my personal favorite). I don't care if you put diamonds *and* pearls on it— it still stays a sow's ear.

When my last husband left, I was devastated, but then I slowly began to see what others had been aware of all along. I won't go into a barrage of attacks on him, but after our breakup, my old boyfriend's words kept coming back to me: "The world called you." So I just told myself that the planet and the people in it are my love affairs—as it should be for you, too. Get rid of your elephant in the front room, throw out the sow's ear, and go out on a crusade to find someone you can love . . . because it will come—maybe not in the person you want, but in so many truly loyal and meaningful ways. Passion is great but fleeting, while true love is everlasting and constant.

Love your friends, the grocer who helps you with an extra good cut of meat, and the old lady whose eyes light up when she sees that you've come to visit her at the nursing home. Love your children, your friends, and your pets. . . . Love spills out everywhere, and if you put it in the right places, it will come back to you a thousandfold. The world is full of things of every size and shape to be loved, including people of all creeds and colors, sunsets, animals, nature, or even the first cup of coffee in the morning. When you've been hurt, start with the small, and then grow spiritually into bigger things.

Children love unconditionally (at least most of them do) until the world gets a hold on them. But from birth to death, pets give out a pure form of unconditional love— they love you no matter who you are or how you look or feel. Humankind could certainly learn from animals! And while it may seem that children and animals are the only sources of unconditional love, I *have* also seen rare instances of it in human relationships.

So you can love and not be loved back or lose your love, but I promise you that, just like it did with me, someone or something will fill its place if you're not too blind to see. The life you live goes in circles that widen, and if you let it, it will take in more people to love. (Don't forget that you can have a wonderful love affair with the teachings of Christ, Mother or Father God, or your guides and angels, too.)

* * * * * *

TENET III

Do not give unto God any human pettiness such as vengeance, wrath, or hate. Negativity is man's alone.

This third tenet is especially dear to my heart. I have researched it, logically gone over it, and seen it in action as miracles, but it really just comes down to plain ol' street smarts.

Where does one begin, I asked myself almost 40 years ago, *to try to explain our Creator, Who has been defamed for centuries?* Christianity is not the only religion responsible for this, although it does seem to be the front-runner. When you look at what its alleged messengers have had to say—and what humankind has made of it—it's just a travesty of lies.

All throughout theological history, humans have viewed God as not only the Creator, but also a Being who played favorites. He was supposedly capricious, jealous, wrathful, and punishing, and He played for favor. He even told Abraham to kill his son (of course, He did later change that desire, but the very fact that God would even ask anyone to kill their son is anathema). When we discover that the God of the Old Testament wanted the Ammonites killed, we have to ask ourselves, "Who made the Ammonites? Why would a loving God even take sides in a war?" God wouldn't, for we all belong to the same genetic family.

Theologians have argued for centuries about this Being called God, and there are as many varied opinions as there are words in the dictionary. Yet one logical truth keeps resounding in the hearts and souls of humankind: Is God vengeful or loving? Let's say for the sake of argument that we've never studied this subject, but we just know that we were created by God. Even with that simplistic premise, the logical question is: *Why would a Creator Who made us condemn us to a life of suffering and hell?* (Granted, life *is* hell, but coming here helps us learn and perfect.) Whatever religious text we read, we still find that God can be good *and* bad—so which is it?

Let's not go into the theological areas here; instead, we'll just go with plain, honest logic. For example, whenever I've sat down with any religious leader, no matter what Supreme Being they follow, I always start out with these questions: "Isn't God good? Isn't God all-loving? Isn't God omnipotent? Isn't God all-forgiving? Isn't God perfect love?" And the answer to all of these questions is, of course, yes. "Okay, then," I tend to respond, "how can He/She be mean, hateful, and capricious?" The silence from these ministers, priests, clerics, rabbis, and theologians has always been deafening. (Although one had the nerve to say to me around 1989 that God must have an evil side in order to create evil. I hit the proverbial roof! God can *know about* evil, but didn't *create* it. Total perfection is what God is about.)

Most of this concept of fearing God and "my god is better than your god" is from the Old Testament of the Bible, which is basically a history of the Judaic people. The Bible was formed to show ancient humans that our deity was stronger than any of the pagan gods of Babylon, Egypt,

Greece, and especially Rome. All of these ancient gods had human qualities (for example, Zeus could rape women and Isis played favorites), and you made sacrifices to all of them to gain favor. Yet sacrifices were also made quite often to God in the Old Testament.

Now I've always had a hard time understanding why Christianity insists on embracing the Old Testament (other than perhaps because it presented a history of Christ's lineage), since it certainly portrays a Creator of human emotions Who is in direct contradiction to the type of God that Christ taught about. Well, the reason this text is embraced is because the early Christian church included it in its holy books. Apparently, it doesn't matter that the Old Testament really doesn't belong in the Bible—especially since a lot of it is part of the Judaic holy scriptures and books. To get it right, the New Testament should be the Christian Bible, but then most Christians don't know the history of how their Bible came into being—or, for that matter, the history of the early Christian church that compiled it.

Anyway, no matter how you portray Him, God has always been constant, loving, and perfect. Once we were all created from good by God, Who gave us free will, and we all made our own choices. So if we have a loving God, then we logically have to stay with that—we can't waffle. Once we grasp this logical, well-founded concept, then we're in league with the God Whom Christ loved and followed, and we can see as he did the hypocrisy and pettiness of humankind. Then we, as Christ said, become the temple in which God resides without vengeance, hate, jealousy, or pettiness.

Many religions seem to try to make their personal god more powerful, intelligent, and even more vengeful. They don't do this out of meanness or spite—fear is actually the common component of the ancient religious teacher's philosophy. You see, Carmelite nuns sequestered themselves in convents to pray for the world, while holy men have sat on mountains to atone for the world for centuries. Please believe me when I say that none of this is wrong—it's each person's individual preference as to how to worship God. I just find it interesting that when you read so many of these antiquated scripts, no messenger ever comes forth and says that this is the law. In other words, it doesn't make sense to have people believe that the only way to achieve redemption is to wear hair shirts, beat themselves bloody, or what have you. How can a loving God want you to mar the temple He/She created in His/Her image and likeness?

I always encourage everyone to read *all* the great religious works—not just our Christian Bible, but the Baha'i *Thief in the Night,* the Talmud, the Koran (Qur'an), and Buddha's Eightfold Path as well. In these varied texts, to make your god more powerful and make your religion prosper, it seems that love was left out, and fear, rules, and dogma reigned supreme. Well, do people today take into account the fact that these early writings were basically for an ignorant mass of people who were continually at war and changing religions to that which was most expedient—namely, the one practiced by the conquering nation?

The uneducated can always be controlled by fear, for they have no knowledge or grasp of the basic concepts related to God. This ruling of the masses by fear led to a tradition that's been carried out to this day: ruling *educated* masses by fear. It's so inbred now in major religions that even a highly educated person, who logically knows that much of what he or she is being taught by their practiced religion makes no sense, still falls into the trap and follows blindly because so many others do.

The role of fear in religion plays on the insecurity of humankind. We're afraid because we categorically don't know who's right or wrong. We seek solace and comfort in the fact that there's a full cathedral, church, mosque, or synagogue—after all, if so many people believe in this practiced religion and attend, then they must be right. Religious leaders know this; consequently, they try to convert as many as possible to their own belief. Truth is thrown out the window, for what has worked for centuries is still working, although there are more and more people who are starting to think for themselves and leaving organized religion in droves. Most of them still believe in God, but they can't abide the stupid rules and dogma that's been handed down for centuries and makes no connection in the modern world . . . especially in light of recent research and just good ol' common sense.

I don't want to pick on any religion, but at one point, if a Catholic ate meat on Friday and died on Saturday, he or she went to hell. Then the law was changed—but what happened to those who'd already gone to hell? Were they told to come back up? Why would God even care what we ate? The Old Testament has David and Solomon partaking in grand feasts, and the New Testament has Jesus being entertained and fed grandly at the house of Martha and Mary . . . nowhere does it say that if it was Friday, no one could have meat. I know I'm oversimplifying what was originally considered a "sacrifice of abstinence" for God, but it was a stupid part of human-made dogma. This was only eliminated a few decades ago—what in the hell took them so long to change it? Tradition and the refusal to change are the bane of all religions. (I don't even want to go into the fact that this particular church only allows men to be priests, for they're not alone in that overt discrimination.)

I'm not particularly in favor of tattoos for myself, but I do feel that it's an individual's right or preference to have them. The Torah prohibits Jews from getting tattoos, which is why Hitler tattooed numbers on concentration-camp victims. Yet we hear of monks or even nuns sleeping on beds of nails or flaying or gouging themselves until their skin is scarred and mutilated, punishing themselves for unworthiness or some sin that they felt they'd committed. Why would God want you to harm yourself—or be accountable for what an evil madman would do to people who had no choice? When your intellect and logic start to work, it can really make you so confused (and even half crazy) trying to sort it out.

We come here to acquire knowledge by making up our charts and learning for God. Think of it like this: God is all-knowing, because He/She knows that to experience is part of knowledge. We (His/Her creations) are the experiencing side of God—not only do we learn for ourselves, but we feed data back to our Creators.

* * *

More times than I can number, people have asked me, "Why is God doing this to me?" First of all, be reasonable—God doesn't play Russian roulette with our lives. And even in an inverted-ego scenario, why would you or I be so important that God just picks on us; or, for that matter, so good that we find favor in becoming a martyr? We need the true presence of a good God, not a critical one.

Every day when I do readings, I seem to hear: "God took my son [daughter, husband, or what have you]" or "I'm mad at God." Don't get me wrong—being human, you can get angry at our Creator. Even though it's useless, sometimes it's as the saying goes: "We always strike out at those we love." Well, the Almighty is no exception. I've had some real screaming matches with God. When a dog bit my granddaughter's lip, I have to say that I gave God a piece of my mind. Angelia's lip is all right, but at the time I had so much fear for her, and I was completely frustrated because I was hundreds of miles away. When my intellect kicked in, I realized it was her chart at work—then my spiritual knowledge chimed in, and I realized that I can't control the destiny of others.

God doesn't take offense, because He/She doesn't have the human pettiness to get mad or hold grudges. Time is the great teacher, and when you look back, nine times out of ten, tragedy turns into greatness, even if it means that you grow spiritually . . . which is what it's all about anyway.

Not long ago, for instance, I was counseling a woman about her three-year-old who had died (the most horrible thing anyone can go through is the loss of a child), and she wailed, "Why did God take my son? What did I ever do so wrong in this life or a past one to incur this?" The answer is simply . . . nothing! In situations like this, we tend to automatically feel that we've failed somehow, and we wonder why bad things happen to good people. This pill is unbearably bitter, and we're often unable to swallow it—until we realize that our loved one didn't die in vain. But how do we figure this out?

As I told my client, "Aside from the unbearable pain, has the death of your child led you anywhere?"

"I don't know what you mean," she said.

I replied, "Isn't that why you're starting to read and search or even call me?"

She was quiet for a moment. Then, as if a light suddenly went on, she said, "Sylvia, I have. I've started searching for answers."

I said, "Well, that's the big first step toward learning about spirituality."

My grandmother's son Paul died when he was a young man, yet she still talked to him every day of her life. She'd tell me (God love her), "If it wasn't for you, Sylvia, I'd love to be with him." She knew she would someday, but she said, "I have to see you on your way." Not until I was 18 did she let go and "graduate." I wasn't ready to let her go (are we ever?), but I can see that she saw me through the developing years of my strange family life, and she helped me face my psychic ability.

You see, if a loved one dies and you just give up, their death hasn't been in vain because they completed and learned from their chart, but it will be in vain for *your* learning process. This "why me" has a definite answer: You simply chart to learn, and the toughest things tend to be left until the last life or incarnation. I used to wonder why, but logically it makes sense that we pick the hardest tasks to learn from, and then graduate so that we don't have to come back into life. At the same time, we also carry a greater amount of accumulated knowledge in the soul to deal with these tragedies.

"Will I see my beloved again?" is also a question I receive quite a bit. Yes, all of us meet each other again because (you guessed it) we have a loving God who allows us to learn and gain a higher understanding, and to even ascend to a higher level of spirituality on the Other Side.

So, if we have an all-loving God, He/She then truly loves us, forgives us, and is always with us. Yes, He/She can interfere with our learning, but does not because we contracted to do it. Does that mean prayer to this loving, perfect God is useless since everything is in its order and place? Of course not! It helps elevate us to God, bringing about grace and a deeper spiritual understanding that at best life is short (sometimes I feel that it's actually very long), but it gives us time to fine-tune our souls.

You and I are partners with God in this journey of life. You might ask, "Why doesn't God always answer prayers?" He/She does, but often has to turn down your pleas—not out of malice or pettiness, but because it would be against your learning curve. It's much like telling your school counselor that you don't want to take speech and calculus, and then being told, "That's fine, but you won't graduate."

So when you feel yourself abandoned, just know that you're not. God holds you forever in the palm of His/Her hand. God loves all people of all creeds, colors, sexes, and religions. How could He/She not—didn't He/She make all of us? If God plays favorites, then here we go with a humanized God. . . .

How Can This Tenet Help You?

Remember that if you're obsessed with the idea of retribution, then it's like the ancient proverb says: "When you go for vengeance, you had better dig two graves: one for you, and one for the person you go after." It may seem that evil prevails sometimes, but it doesn't. You just might not see the justice you're seeking in this life, for it will be done in God's time, not yours. Evildoers have to keep coming back until they're finally absorbed into God, while we keep our own identity as a shining example of His/Her goodness.

We've got to get back to the basics of loving God and accepting His/Her never-ending love for us. God is love, and that love doesn't hurt, is never cruel, and accepts us for the sum total of who we are and who we were made to be—rather than what religion's human-made rules have placed upon us. If we just followed what Jesus taught and did, then we'd be on our spiritual, simplistic track and love the God Who is gentle, kind, and omnipotent.

Everyone has searched for the right God, and He/She has always been there for us . . . always constant, always forgiving, and always loving. If we just stick with how Jesus addressed his Creator—and know and love God as our Father/Mother Who is not only in heaven, but always with us—then we're guaranteed to be on the spiritual path.

* * * * * *

TENET IV

Create your own heaven, not a hell.
You are a creator made from God.

I know that at times this book may seem more like a self-indulgent autobiography rather than a text on spiritual-ity. This is partly because I'm sharing what these 21 tenets have helped me learn from my own life, but I'm also includ-ing what I've learned from *your* lives. To prove that point, I have to tell you about Sister Francis.

At the time (40 years ago), I was working at St. Albert the Great, teaching second grade. Sister Francis was a fel-low instructor, and we'd try to spend our free time between classes or at lunch together. That always meant going out-doors, because Sister Francis dearly loved to be out in nature. She and I would go out rain or shine, and she never failed to say, "What a beautiful day this is! Look at the splendor God has laid out before us!"

At first I thought she was exaggerating, but gradually I began to see what she saw: the variances in temperature, the cloud formations, the soft beat of the rain, and even the cold that made your face pink and flushed when you came back inside. Sister Francis truly had heaven in her own mind.

Then there was my grandfather, Marcus Coil, who'd become a millionaire in Springfield, Missouri, by starting up some of the town's first laundries and mercantile stores. By the time the family had moved to Kansas City, however, he'd lost every penny in the stock market. Although it was during the time of the Great Depression, every day my grandfather would press his now-shiny-with-wear suit and shirt (which Grandma Ada had to keep repairing the frayed cuffs on) and sit in the waiting room of Pacific Gas and Electric looking for work. And every day, the head of the company would come out and say, "Sorry, Marcus, we have nothing for you today."

For one year my grandfather followed this routine. Finally, the CEO told my grandpa that he was sick of seeing him every day and that anyone who had that type of perseverance deserved a job. My grandfather was given a menial position, but in six months he became the head of the whole district office. He kept telling Grandma Ada, "I made it once; I know how to do it again." Was this all about money? God, no—it was about providing for his family and taking a positive and undaunted attitude. My grandfather was able to create a heaven out of his hell.

On the other side of this coin you have my mother. It's hard to understand how she could have come from the same family as my wonderful grandparents, her brother Marcus (who had cerebral palsy but was an angel on Earth whom everyone called "Brother"), and her brother Paul, who was also psychic and used to talk to God daily before he died of cancer at the age of 21. Out of this family of beloved people came my mother. I used to obsess about not liking her until Francine told me many years later, "You can only honor your parents if they are honorable."

My mother was not only abusive physically, but her

greatest forte was to try to damage her family members with mental abuse. I was too tall, not pretty, and too strong willed. I also thought I was smart, even when she told me I wasn't—this seemed to set a fire in my gut to make her wrong. I was also my father's favorite, which endeared me to her even less.

Now I could have wilted under her abuse and become like her, but instead I went under my beloved grandma's wing and basked in the light of my dad's approval. My poor sister, Sharon, wasn't so fortunate, however: My mother got her claws into her and for a time controlled her and almost made her an invalid. To this day, my mother's influence has affected my sister's life—and not in a positive way. (You can say that I was stronger, and that may be so, but I also chose my chart.)

Being psychic didn't help me in my mother's eyes, even though she'd grown up with a psychic mother, brother, grandmother, and uncle. With all due respect, she may have had enough of it, but instead of encouraging me as Grandma Ada did, when I was ten years old, she told me, "Keep this spooky thing up and I'll have you locked up." I can remember being so frightened that night that I could hear my heart beat through the bed, and I truly prayed that my gifts would go away.

When I hesitantly told my grandmother about the incident, I remember her listening carefully and getting a grim look on her face. She silently put on her coat and grabbed my hand, and we both marched off to see my mother. Now this was one of only two times I saw my grandmother get angry in the 18 years that I was with her. Seething with anger, she went up to my mother, put her face close to hers, and said, "Celeste, if you ever say that to Sylvia again, I'll personally see to it that *you* are locked up!" So that ended that . . . except for the constant snorts and sighs of disapproval my mother directed toward me over the years whenever I'd do mini-readings for friends or come out with a zinger of psychic insight.

My psychic ability was even accepted by my childhood friends (who will attest to it). In fact, I recently attended my 50th high-school reunion, and my classmates all told me they were proud of me. Even the nuns and priests, believe it or not, were good to me back then—while they didn't always understand how I knew what I knew, they never condemned me. In fact, all throughout Catholic high school and college, and even during the 18 years that I taught in Catholic schools, I was never made to feel that I was evil or an oddity. At Presentation High School in San Jose, California, they even let me teach world religions, which I have to confess had Gnosticism on the agenda more than the Bible, Bhagavad Gita, Koran, or Talmud. Of course I gave time to all of these, but I kept coming back to a loving God and the fact that life is what we make of it inside our soul . . . because, after all, that's where our heaven and hell reside.

Getting back to my childhood, as I grew into my late teens, my father was making $3,000 a month. That was a fortune in those days, so I didn't have an underprivileged upbringing in those years, but I truly would have foregone that for a semblance of a happy home. Yet I can honestly say that I was happy overall because I had the rest of my family and my friends. I chose to respect my mother, while at the same time putting her on a shelf in the back of my mind.

During this time, my grandmother fell on hard times. My grandfather had died, and Grandma Ada was taking care of Brother. It's very difficult for me to relive this portion of my memories, for my mother stuck them both in a literal flophouse. You may wonder why my father didn't intervene, but it's more unbelievable and complex than that. My father left everything to my mother to handle because he traveled all the time and really didn't know what was going on with my mother's family. I was right there when she lied and told him that no one would take Brother because of his cerebral palsy. Well, she never even looked—nor was she about to spend any of her considerable allowance to have them taken care of.

I remember the day Grandma Ada and Brother moved into this three-flight walk-up that my mother had put them in. Brother was afraid of stairs because his disease threw his balance off, and then a drunk came out brandishing a knife. I think I was so full of grief that I turned on the man and screamed, "Get back in your room before I use that knife on you!" He looked befuddled and stunned. I guess so . . . seeing a 13-year-old girl going into what looked like a manic fit.

I saw that my beloved family members were going to be reduced to living in a dirty one-room flat with a communal bathroom down the hall. I kept thinking, *Please, God, let me grow up fast so that I can take care of them.* The room contained a bed, one straight-back chair, two hot plates, a few large windows with no curtains, a small sink, and a dresser—and that was it. (Oh, except for the two dishes, glasses, and sets of eating utensils; along with a pair of sheets and a flimsy blanket, plus two pillows and towels that my extravagant mother had so thoughtfully provided.) This is what my grandmother—who was of German nobility, escaped the war, gave to charity, healed the sick, and helped as many people as she could—had been given by her own daughter.

Grandma Ada sat down on the chair, and for a moment I saw what looked like a cloud cross her china-blue eyes. But then she threw her hat on the bed and sat down. Then, like my granddaughter, Angelia, still does, I flung myself on my grandmother's lap—all 13 years of me. She must have seen my pain because she said, "Look at those windows! Brother can look out every day and see the sights, and we'll have light all day long." She patted me and said, "It'll be just fine, darling. I'll make it great in no time."

I'd like to take a moment here to talk a little bit more about Brother, who lived with my grandmother until her death at age 88. He was one of the most brilliant people I've ever known. He read everything—history, religion, politics, you name it—and could talk about it. He was very frail, with reddish hair and blue eyes, and stood only about 5'8". His head was tilted to one side because of his cerebral palsy, and his neck would bob violently when he was agitated or nervous. When I walked down the street with him and people stared (as they're wont to do), I glared at them, silently daring them to say one word.

When she was asked about how hard it was to take care of him, my grandmother, without hesitation, would say, "Are you kidding? Look what joy and company I have in my older years—we have fun, read, talk, and laugh; and without him, I'd be alone. How can this blessing be a burden?" Once again, as you can see, out of a hell (or what's perceived to be one) lies a heaven in disguise.

My grandmother never really read for me because we couldn't for each other, but she did say that I'd have two boys, would go to California, and that people would know my name. "Me, a girl from Missouri? I think not! And how will they know my name?" I pressed her.

She replied, "You'll carry the torch that was built upon itself for 300 years." *How poetic,* I'd think, but then I rationalized that she loved me so much she was blinded by it. In fact, in a half-kidding way I once asked her while we were cooking, "Grandma, how much do you love me?"

She stopped what she was doing, looked at me, and said, "My heart would hear you and beat if it lay for a century dead." Now try to top that one!

My grandmother was a writer, too, and someday I'm going to publish her letters. Every one is filled with quotes, all of which were gloriously optimistic. She *always* made a heaven out of a living hell. For example, in that room that she and Brother shared, she got ahold of some donated fabric and made a skirt for the dresser and one for the sink to hide the utensils and dishes, and she made another sheet for the bed . . . but it was still a rattrap.

When my father came home two weeks later, I immediately went to him and tried to explain how awful it was. He had some business issue on his mind, so I could tell he wasn't with me. My mother came in and said, "Bill, don't listen to her—she's always so dramatic anyway. You can go see for yourself what a cozy place this is," knowing full well that he wouldn't. He either wanted to believe her or was afraid not to, I'll never know. I do know that after that, he'd slip me money to take to Grandma.

I can remember on more than one occasion skipping school with money in my pocket, taking the streetcar in the blinding snow to 18th and Baltimore, and walking up to that damn run-down building. I'd look up and see a form in the window, standing there with that Gibson-girl hairstyle she had, smiling and waving because she psychically knew that I was coming (after all, she had no phone). I'd climb the steps and give her the money, prompting her to clap her hands together, tell me what a good man my father was, and remark that we were going to have a feast. That meant a soda, cheese, milk, and hamburger stew.

As painful as it was, Grandma could even light up a dingy cell-like room with love and joy. She'd always say, "Isn't this cozy?" or "Aren't we lucky?" or "Aren't we happy to have each other?" I decided to believe her. And it didn't take long for people to again find out where she was. Long lines began to form to see her—priests, laypeople, old people, and sick people . . . she'd see everyone. I used to say, "God, please let me just be one-tenth as strong, brave, and positive as she is throughout *my* life."

Well, I won't lie or be humble, but I can't honestly say that I've arrived at the point that my grandparents or Sister Francis reached, but I try valiantly. I *can* say that when I got divorced from my abusive first husband, Gary, and was relegated to tenement living (where there was algae all over the pool in back), I told my boys that it was just water lilies. However, after two ear infections, I decided that enough was enough.

Not only did I have Paul and Chris, I also had my adopted daughter, Mary, whose mother had simply given her to me when the child was only 6. (Mary left us when she was 22 and is now married with two girls and living near Boston.) And I was so strung out at the time with my ex-husband's threats to kill us that I didn't know if I was coming or going. The police actually told me that Gary could stand on the sidewalk in a threatening manner and there was nothing I could do about it. One officer said that the only way I could stop Gary would be to pull him into our apartment and shoot him. Since I could never ever hurt anyone or anything in that way, that wasn't a viable option either.

Yet, even through this horrendous period, the kids and I managed to scrape by. People were so caring. For example, when Chris had a terrible earache (the attack of the "water lilies"), the woman next door came over with what I deem were no less than magical drops for his ear—and he was fine from then on. Mary was a love, and together, even at her age, we'd laugh about all the pork and beans we ate.

At this same time, my mother went to a lawyer to try to get my children. My lawyer was flabbergasted: Here I was, a Catholic schoolteacher and a good mother, and she was going after custody with my ex-husband. The reason, she explained later, was that she didn't want to lose us. *Huh?*

At one point in my late 20s and early 30s, as I was raising the kids by myself, teaching school, doing readings, *and* attending classes, I began to see that my life wasn't going the way I wanted it to. It felt like an endless circle of readings, teaching, raising children, school, and nothing else. Then I began to ask myself, "What do *you* want, Sylvia?"

I really wanted to teach and help people, but I also needed to give the children a good home. So I quit my job as a schoolteacher and opened my foundation. We had two rooms and taught classes in the evenings, and I brought my kids with me. They'd sit in the back and do their homework—then we'd go to Denny's, eat dinner, and talk about everything. Sure, finances were really tough, but the trade-off was great. It was the process of selection: I had my family with me because when they were in school I did readings in my home, and three nights a week, they went with me to lectures or teaching.

Life went on and on . . . it can take on a Shakespearean quality (or even a comedy of errors), but you roll with it. Life also gives you grief and sorrow in large measures: It can deceive and disappoint you, but it also gives you happiness; ecstasy; satisfaction; and loving friends, pets, and family— all part of the montage that makes your life how you perceive it: a joy.

When my third husband, Larry, exited three years ago, things became quite difficult. I like having partnership at this point in my life, but I also feel that people my age or even younger should find fulfillment by doing what they feel is right, not what society dictates. Anyway, right in the middle of the divorce, Dal Brown (my second husband whose name I still carry, although I added an *e* to it) showed up at my office and told me that he was getting an amicable divorce from his wife of two years. He was working as a store manager in Auburn, California, and had come to the Bay Area on business when he decided out of the blue to stop by and see me. His children had moved away, and we talked about old times. We'd kept in touch sporadically since our divorce, and one thing led to another. . . .

Although Dal has had many serious health problems (including heart trouble and several operations that left him on disability for a while), shortly after both our divorces were final we decided to become companions for one another. After all, I'd known him for almost 40 years, and we had 18 years of marriage together. All the old hurts were forgotten—what he'd done with our finances had been out of stupidity, not malicious intent. So we're friends . . . and even though he doesn't share any part of my business, it's nice to have someone around who knows me. He has his life, and I have mine, but we try to spend as much time as we can with each other.

As you can see, with the closing of one door, another opens. Even though I was hurt by my last divorce, I found solace in the fact that there was so much good in my life. These days, my perfect setting is coming home from being on the road and sitting next to the fireplace with Angelia, needlepointing and talking, while my grandson Willy plays with his toy trucks, with a stew on the stove that we can eat whenever we want.

And then I feel all the loved ones who have passed over—Dad, Grandma Ada, and Brother; my dear friend Dr. Small, who was always there for me if I couldn't pay the medical bills for my children; Bob Williams, my mentor, friend, and teacher whom I dearly loved; Joe, who was one of my first loves; Abass, who was my friend and tour guide in Egypt (and when I was going through my last divorce would call me every day and ask, "How are you doing, Queenie?" [his nickname for me]); and myriad other souls who have passed on. I know that they're all there with Francine and the angels, and the room fills up with love. That's when I tell myself, "This is your heaven right here, Sylvia."

How Can This Tenet Help You?

As Milton said, "The mind is its own place, and in itself can make a Heav'n of Hell." When things used to happen to my children and me that were wonderful, I'd always say, "Close your eyes and save it, because when things go wrong on that awful, dark, rainy day that life gives you, you can take this out—like a scrapbook of your life. Cherish this moment, and it will brighten even your darkest hour."

Sometimes it's better not to act at all during the hard times—instead, stay in your quiet, spiritual place, and reach for God's hand that's always there. Can you look at yourself in the mirror? Can you sleep at night? If so, then you're okay. I don't mean that you won't lose sleep over the pain, grief, and whys of life, but did you pull the bow that sent the arrow? I doubt it—or you wouldn't be reading this (or any other) spiritual commentary or text because you wouldn't care. It's only good people who worry whether they're on track—the bad ones never do.

Take the people you know who are rich or famous, only to find out that they have substance abuse, broken marriages, eating disorders, and so forth. Money and fame don't exempt you from problems. Look at Martha Stewart: Right or wrong, she stumbled, and created a hell for herself. Then again, Montel Williams, one of the guardian angels of my life, battles multiple sclerosis (MS), but he keeps on going and finds joy. He goes snowboarding, travels, helps people, started an MS foundation, and is proactive. He's stumbled but hasn't fallen. There was a time, which he himself even wrote about, when he found himself in his own hell and wanted to end it all, but from deep in his soul came the strength to live, love, and enjoy every day.

How can we take for granted the feeling of capturing a child's hand in ours, looking into a baby's eyes, or seeing the joy on our pets' faces when we come home? What about the ardent kiss of a lover, a sunset or sunrise, a bird's song . . . there's so much beauty that we don't even notice because we get rooted in our own hell. Remember that there's always going to be a hole in the prison walls that you construct for yourself—why do you think you have the desire if your chart didn't put it there? Stop with the "I'm too old, too young, not equipped, not smart enough," for then you'll create your own hell. It's not your dreams that you're worried about following, but your destiny!

Not only do you need passion as you realize your path, but you've also got to prepare and steel yourself against the "slings and arrows of outrageous fortune." It's true that bravery comes with a price, but know that you're building on your mistakes and heartaches. Rejoice that you're not only climbing the mountain of self, but you're also learning to love unconditionally—as well as giving yourself to an all-loving God. And *that's* where you'll find your heaven on Earth.

❋ ❋ ❋ ❋ ❋ ❋

TENET V

*Turn thy power outward, not inward,
for therein shines the light and the way.*

As opposed to the last tenet, which was internal (creating heaven instead of hell), this one is proactive and more external. Of course, power must start inside—if there isn't anything in there, it's pretty difficult to turn the "power light" on, especially when the cord isn't plugged into anything. Sometimes it's best to just take a moment and decide if we're feeling happy or dull, with no passion that can propel us outward in our lives. Think about it rationally: Our eyes don't turn inward but outward to see; our bodies even fit into other bodies. In other words, we weren't built as mere receiving tubes, but as entities that were made to focus out.

When we turn outward, then as the tenet says, therein shines the light and the way. The light means spiritual enlightenment, while the way is following the teachings of Christ. As our Lord said, "I am the light of the world." He, of course, was very spiritually enlightened and certainly didn't sit around—rather, he chose to focus his power outward. He walked and talked, taught and healed.

Now Francine has always said that we all have more power than we could ever realize or know until we use it. At first this made me crazy. "Okay, then," I asked her, "where is it and how do we use it?" When she told me to look at the concept deeper, it became clear that it was related to miracles.

For example, I know of a mother and two children who were wedged in a car after an accident, and the car caught fire. There was no way that anyone could see how the fire department with their "jaws of life" could get there in time before they'd be engulfed by flames. As everyone stood around screaming, a beautiful black man came out of the crowd, approached the car, and with one hand ripped the door off its hinges and saved the mother and children. Everyone there reported that the man had a trancelike look on his face the whole time he was executing the rescue. I stated at one point that this man was an angel, but I now believe that the angels actually propelled his power outward instead. When the man was subsequently found after a long, intensive search, he had no recollection of the episode—but even more startling was the discovery that four years prior to that episode (almost to the day), he'd lost his wife and two children in a house fire and felt helpless because he wasn't home to save them.

Then there's the story of the 90-pound mother who actually lifted a huge SUV off of her son, who was pinned underneath it. He came out with just a concussion and a broken leg, but authorities said that if the SUV had been left on top of the boy, he would have suffered internal injuries due to the weight of the vehicle. Many say that the woman's strength came from a rush of adrenaline, but it doesn't mat-ter—there was a surge of power that defied all explanation. You can call this the energy that always comes from God, but it's actually lying beneath the surface in all of us and can be used when called upon by a desperate need to save, heal, or simply make a situation better.

The power that we can exude physically when needed is truly a miracle in itself. I remember about 40 years ago when a friend and her four-year-old daughter, Sally, were visiting. My kids were playing with the little girl and were just coming down the stairs when out of the corner of my eye I saw Sally fall. I was on the couch, which was far away from the steps. Without thinking, I jumped up and with one leap managed to catch her head before it hit the last step. In wide-eyed disbelief, Sally's mother proclaimed, "I never saw anything like that! You were like a blur of motion, and your reflexes were miraculous." I'm not being heroic or humble here—I'm sure I was simply propelled by a primordial God-given reflex to save this child from possible brain damage, which surely would have occurred had she hit her head at the rate she was falling.

I happened recently to tune in to a show called *Extreme Makeover: Home Edition,* in which a home was remodeled for a family that had two deaf parents and two sons, one of whom was blind. After the house was completed, the blind son was lifted up so that he could ring the wind chimes, which brought him such joy to hear. The other son was given money for the college education he so dearly wanted.

The family was in tears, and the show's host said, "It gave me such a sense of power and grace from God." This coming from someone on a reality show! I thought, *We're finally getting it. It's even sinking into mainstream America that we do have the power to change lives.* Sure, we don't all have that kind of money on a grand scale or the physical powers, but we do have the power to heal. Maybe we won't attain the level of Padre Pio, a famous priest who was known for his healing ability, but we all hold the potential.

* * *

How can we "ordinary people" do outward healing? Well, each and every one of us has the energy to do it—and it can be physical as well as mental. For example, the prefect of our church had a daughter named Kathy who had a very advanced case of multiple sclerosis. Since she was also one of our ministers, many naysayers would ask Kathy, "Why are you not healed?"

I'll never forget her response: "What you don't understand is that I have been. Just because my body has MS doesn't mean that my soul isn't at peace or that I don't know the truth of where I'm going and why I came here." In other words, Kathy *was* healed.

Now don't get me wrong: It's important to address physical concerns, but when the mind and soul are convinced of its spiritual path and light, it *is* healed. Just as we aren't the car we drive—we just operate and then exit it—we aren't the physical shell we inhabit.

Think of the power of any emotion, and watch what it can accomplish. Love can almost move mountains; unfortunately, so can hate and vengeance. I truly love my life now, even though it took many years to keep that power steady. There were periods when I loved it and times that were heartbreaking and dismal with death, divorce, and betrayal, but you know what? I found out that as we constantly reach toward our passion, our power gets stronger, and it's that power that's turned outward.

When I was 18 years old and doing readings, I was happy. And when I was teaching and raising my children, I was happy. It was in those other outside things like holding on to bad memories of my childhood, a bad marriage, or the death of a loved one (which has happened to me many times), that my light would dim because it was focused inside on the deadly trap of "poor me." One day I finally told myself, "You can stay in this comfortable circle, or you can go for broke. If you don't go for it, how will you ever know what you can accomplish?"

So with trepidation I started to go public. The same thing happened when I wanted to start Novus Spiritus—my family just sat in stunned silence. My boys spoke up first and said, "Mom, it's always been your ball game, so play it." It was hard, and the criticism was even harder, but I kept putting one foot in front of the other and praying that this was what God wanted.

I gain power from writing and from all of you—fans of my books, those who come to my lectures, the people I read for—as well as from doing shows for Montel or Larry King (who is a prince and the best interviewer in the world). Whenever Larry sees me, he starts to quote Shakespeare: "Who is Sylvia? What is she? That all our swains commend her . . ."

Will I ever retire? Never! It really sounds disgusting to me that the root of that word is *tire*. Plus, what do we really do when we retire? People say, "I'll do all the things I always wanted to do," and then I ask, "Such as . . . ?" knowing full well what's coming. "Oh, I'll sleep as late as I want, watch all the TV shows I've missed, read, visit with friends," is the response I typically get. Well, then what? How many books can you read? I read and write all the time—in fact, I usually have three books going at once. I also watch my favorite shows on A&E or the Discovery and History Channels, and I love to needlepoint. I do all of these things and still go out and do what I love with all of you.

I think we should get rid of the four-letter word *work*. The idea of work is what causes us to lose our power and passion to turn outward. If it turns inward, it lies dormant, is useless, and doesn't go anywhere.

Take, for example, my dear friend Lindsay's mother. She's in her late 80s, yet she teaches a children's Bible class, takes kids on educational field trips, and was recently honored for her contribution to society. She hurt her back a few years ago and couldn't wait to get better so that she could get back to her "little people" (which is what I used to call my students when I taught). Then she got pneumonia, but she willed herself to get better and was up faster than any doctor could predict at her age. She didn't fall into the pit of "pneumonia is the old people's friend"; instead, her one focus was to get to her children. Her passion—that is, her power going outward—healed her.

* * *

I don't think that we can leave this tenet without the actual extension of righteousness and justice that it deserves. A perfect example of this happened when I was 16. My father had a mistress named Virginia who lived three blocks from us. My mother knew about it, but because she liked the economic lifestyle she was getting used to, she closed her mind to it. I know that I've said that "it takes two," but I'd been an unhappy witness to my mother's castrating ways. She was very moody and stayed in her room for days, where she'd usually lie around in a leopard-skin robe and read. My sister, Sharon, was left with me and our maid, Rosie, who had been with us for years. Poor Rosie was hardly ever paid—yes, my mother gave her carfare and food, but she always told my father that she paid her. My dad would end up paying Rosie when he would get home from business trips—each time he usually had to give her back pay as well.

Anyway, Daddy said that he was going to leave and when he got settled he'd send for me. As much as I loved my father, I couldn't leave Sharon or Grandma Ada and Brother. The thought of either being with my father and Virginia or of staying with my mother and being relegated to the keeper of the household was more than I could bear.

At the time I was dating one of the sweetest guys in the world, and I confided to him how torn up I was. Joe looked at me for a long time and said, "Why don't we get married? Then I could stay and help you." I thought it was the perfect solution! I'd be married; even at his age he was working two jobs, so I felt I'd be taken care of. (And we loved each other.) We were too young to get married in Missouri or Kansas, but I had a brainstorm: If I doctored up our birth certificates, we could go to Kansas and finish our senior year, and no one would be the wiser.

It was September 16th (I'll never forget the day!), and I dressed in a white pinafore with matching white sandals. Joe met me at the streetcar, with two of our friends whom we'd sworn to secrecy. We got off in Kansas City, Kansas, and Joe and I had to get a blood test, which resulted in me almost fainting. Nevertheless, we marched to the courthouse and got married.

As soon as we were done, I became physically ill—not because I didn't love him, but thanks to that gut-level feeling of *What have I done, and really, what was the reason I did it?* Yet Francine assured me, "You'll see how this will play out for the best."

I got home at around 3:30 in the afternoon and was going to change because Joe was going to pick me up as if we were going on a date. We'd then "consummate our marriage" . . . which hadn't dawned on me until later when I thought about all the other parts of what being married meant. Well, I walked in the house, and my mother, who never seemed to care about my comings and goings before, asked me where I'd been.

It was almost as if a silent signal had been sent out. This isn't because I'm so good, but I just couldn't lie. Would you believe I opened my mouth and blurted out, "I just married Joe"?

My mother went into hysterics and went to track down my father. I couldn't face that, so I took a few dollars out of my drawer, caught the streetcar, and went to the local Katz drugstore. I must have sat there for hours drinking Coke after Coke and crying. I kept wondering, *What did I do? How many people have I hurt? What was I thinking?*

I decided to get back on the streetcar and go see my grandmother. I remember it as if it were yesterday: I ran in the door and knelt on the floor with my head in her generous lap, and in between hiccups and crying my eyes out, I told her what I'd done. She didn't say anything for a while— she just listened and rubbed my face and stroked my hair. Sounding like Francine, she kept saying, "It will all turn out all right—nothing ventured, nothing gained."

Finally, the door opened and there was my mother, looking like the mad Lady of Shallot. She looked at me and then at my grandmother, and then she screamed, "Mama, what are we going to do with Sylvia?!"

Without missing a beat, Grandma Ada shot back, "That's not really the question. The question is what are we going to do with *you?*" Apparently this was one of the few times that my grandmother had ever spoken to my mother like that, so she just stood there with her mouth open. My grandmother continued, "Celeste, get your house in order, and for once look outside of yourself," which, of course, goes right back to this tenet we've been discussing.

Well, I didn't know whether I was still upset by what I'd done or more dumbfounded by what I'd witnessed, but I rode home with my mother in silence. When we arrived, my father was there. He had his head in his hands and had been crying. "Daddy," I wailed, "I'm so sorry!"

All he did was ask, "Why, Sylvia?" At this point, I really didn't know why I'd done it. What seemed so clear to me at the time was now just a mishmash of pain, and I felt that I'd been incredibly selfish.

My father promptly got on the phone and called an attorney to have the marriage annulled. This was on a Friday, and I went through Saturday and wouldn't take Joe's calls. On Sunday, I finally told him what had happened. He said, "Where do we go from here?" I truly didn't know. I was so full of shame.

Wouldn't you know that even though Joe and I had gotten married in another state, it had showed up that Sunday in our city's newspaper? I had to go to school the next day, but I didn't sleep all night. After all, this was the early 1950s, and good girls, especially Catholic ones, didn't do this sort of thing.

I'll never forget entering the school—of course, my locker had to be at the end of the hall. Joe hadn't shown up (I found out later he was sick with a high fever), but my dear friend Warren walked right up to me and took my hand. He said, "Walk with me with your head high, and just take one step at a time." The silence was deafening—there were whispers and backs turned. Shaking like a leaf all the way, I made it to my locker. I blindly went to my first class and sat down. Sister Delores quietly said, "Sister Teresa Marie and Father Hicks want to see you in the office."

Here it comes, I thought. I went in repeating to myself, "Within your weakness—or, in this case, your silly selfishness—lies your strength sleeping." First, Father told me to ask forgiveness for what I'd done, and I did. Then Sister Teresa Marie said, "We've decided to keep you, but we're going to send Joe to another school." I pleaded, "No, please don't! I'll go—it wasn't his fault. I more or less talked him into it because of a problem I was having."

"Are you pregnant?" Sister asked.

"Of course not!" I replied, horrified (but now I see why that would have been a logical assumption).

"We'll keep him then if you promise you won't date or hang around him anymore."

"I promise," I said. It hurt so bad because puppy love or not, I really loved him. I never told Joe that they wanted him out, but if he reads this he'll understand.

Time heals. . . . Daddy found out that Virginia was having an affair with another man, and for whatever reason, the family sort of hung together. My father never played around again, and I'm sure he settled into a life of quiet desperation, but we did have some good times and great vacations in California. Grandma Ada was the rock, of course, and by her telling my mother to turn outward, she did try in her own way. It was a moment in time in which my motive was (I thought) pure. At least I tried to do something, and Francine was right . . . everything turned out okay.

I saw Joe again at our 50th class reunion. He walked right up to me, just as he has many times over the years. He's now been married five times and has six kids (I think that, like me, he has a penchant for trying to make people better), and his present wife is an angel and I love her. Anyway, when he walked up, he kissed me and said, "I'll always remember you, sweetheart—you were my first love." I kissed him back and said, "And you were mine." [**Note:** This isn't the Joe who was my boyfriend later on and recently died, whom I mentioned in the Introduction.]

Before we go on to the next tenet, I hope that you can see how life takes its turns, and if you keep going, things do get better—if, that is, you turn outward rather than go in and hide. Just think of my grandmother's words to my mother: *Look outside of yourself.* Sometimes you won't always do the right thing, but if your heart is in the right place, it usually does come out okay.

How Can This Tenet Help You?

Is your power genetic, environmental, or just in your chart? Well, it's a little of all three, but I believe that it's in every human soul to succeed, whether it's a primitive people's need for survival or Dr. Jonas Salk's discovery of the polio vaccine. Let's examine your chart again, as it still might be causing you some confusion. You've written all the major and minor points you need to learn—the bad, the ugly, and the beautiful—but you may not realize that it all comes down to what you make of it. Say that you've written in (as horrible as it sounds) that you lose a child or loved one. While you may have fulfilled that horrendous learning curve, it's what you do with it that brings about spirituality.

So even with your chart, you still can create miracles or make your schooling here so much more enjoyable by literally "putting on a happy soul" and projecting your power outward. You can make yourself as well as you wish to be and have even more physical strength by doing the right things for your body. Physically, it's best to eat healthfully, exercise, and take vitamin supplements; get regular facials or massages; and avoid drugs, alcohol, and nicotine. But what's vitally important—no matter what age you are—is that you believe you're strong, not sickly, fragile, or frail.

Now that we've addressed the outward manifestation of strength and power, I'd like you to realize that not everything comes down to your instinct and survival—it also comes from your soul and even from life, which has hopefully given you the strength to get through any hurdles and sorrows . . . even if your power isn't psychic. Maybe it lies in building a boat or running a small business. The world is filled with options, but we seem to be infected by a type of malaise that threatens our health and creates more mental stress. Every time I hear "I'd like to do it, but I haven't gotten around to it," I always respond, "Do it now! Make the time."

Just keep in mind that when I started to write and share my research, I endured years of scoffing and critical and cruel rhetoric. But if you're full of conviction and walk in truth, you're going to make it, just like I did. So many people can't get out of the box—all I ask is that you try. Believe me, if you do, you'll notice that there's sunshine, fresh air, and blessings all around!

✳ ✳ ✳ ✳ ✳ ✳

TENET VI

In faith be like the wind chimes: Hold steady until faith, like the wind, moves you to joy.

I've often mentioned the desert period in life, which happens to all of us—whether we live in an actual arid region or not. It can happen at the beginning, middle, or end of our days, although most individuals choose the early or middle years because these times are confusing to begin with. We might call it puberty or a midlife crisis, but a desert period can hit whenever we chart it. This is how it operates: We feel that we're just existing or are in a rut. We get up, go to work (or do whatever we have to do) without joy, and then we go to bed.

"What am I going to be?" "Where am I going?" and "What does it all mean?" are common sayings for our early days; and "What have I done?" "What have I accomplished?" "Am I on track?" and "Have I failed?" are common threads of middle age.

Life themes have been written about many times in my

books, but it should be explained that these are actually subjects that we choose to learn from in order to become what God wants us to be. (For a detailed description of our themes, please see my book *Soul's Perfection*.) We don't tend to pick the same themes for each life; rather, we choose different ones that will help us expand our knowledge for God and ourselves. For example, we don't want to become a victim, so we conquer it. Some themes are negative and can belong to the dark side, but we need the negative to accentuate the positive, so to speak: A poverty theme can mean that you can beat it by not succumbing to it. Usually all the themes are for us to learn from and overcome, and within that process we have our desert periods.

Faith to us Gnostics is synonymous with *knowing*, which is really important during the desert period . . . and Lord knows I understand this. When I was around 50, I went through a bad one of these. I'd been doing readings and teaching for years, and although I enjoyed it, it was the sameness of it that was getting me down. I wanted to break out—and that's when Hay House picked up *My Guide, Myself*. I tinkered with it; added to, deleted, and updated it; and renamed it. You might know it as *Adventures of a Psychic* . . . a book that went on *The New York Times* bestseller list and stayed there for more than a year. I then got on the *Montel Williams Show* a few years later, and I've never looked back. When I did feel that I was in the proverbial vicious cycle, I went on the road and lectured, which I still do today because I love it so much. Now I'm taking cruises and lecturing on them, too.

So many times, especially in this day and age, we look at times of inactivity as depression. I'm not talking about people who need pharmaceuticals here, since many of us have chemical imbalances that physiologically as well as biologically cause depression, but we often run for a fast fix instead of realizing that we charted this for ourselves. The word *depressed* means to "press down," and many times it's nature's way of getting us to stop and take stock of our life.

Even what we call "accidents" can be written in our charts to slow us down.

I remember about 15 years ago, for example, when I was running up the steps to my front door and just nicked my right foot on one of the bricks. The next day my foot was twice its size. I went to the doctor and found out I had blood poisoning and cellulitis (all over a little nick in my foot!). I came home with pills and poultices and was relegated to soaking my foot. Thoroughly aggravated, I sat down on the couch and said, "What in the hell is this about?" The message that came in loud and clear was: "You're running too fast—you have to slow down."

So when I find my clients in a desert period, I explain that to have faith, they have to be quiet and hold steady because this truly is the time when they can learn all those miserable lessons they don't want to—the tolerance, the patience, the endurance, and the survival that they never would have learned during the frenzied times. Instead of looking at a desert period as a bad thing, I tell my clients to be still and go through it like a cleansing. This way, when their faith and knowing, like the wind, not only moves them to the joy of what they've accomplished, they'll also be moved to activation.

When unexpected negative change hits, which it does in all lives, we have a tendency to go on hold. The desert period is called this because it can seem like no matter where we look, there's only sand as far as the eye can see. Sometimes we might see a mirage—which is even worse, for it takes the form of a false solution that only sinks us deeper into the sand. So what can we do? We can only keep walking . . . eventually, the heat will subside, and before we know it, we will have reached the oasis.

We always have a choice: We can gripe and cry and shake our fists at the sky and wonder what we've ever done to deserve this long "nothing" period, or we can use it to advance our soul. Think for a moment about how the pioneers felt coming from my area of St. Joseph, Missouri, to

Oregon and California. Now that was a real, living desert period—I mean, think of the heat, the lack of conveniences, the Indian raids, and so forth.

When I was in Egypt, talking to about 250 people in front of the Sphinx and the Great Pyramid, I contemplated what it must be like for the Bedouins who really do live in this rocky wasteland. Then I pictured the ancient caravans that followed the trade routes in the heat and unforgiving sun, while fighting with the bugs, scorpions, and unruly camels (which are amazing and wonderful animals, but God, they smell bad!).

You can say of the Bedouins that they're used to it—well, that's not exactly true. I was privileged to talk to a large group of Arabs near the tomb of Seti I and asked them if they loved their life. In very good English they answered, "Madam, it is a life. It is very hard and many get sick and die, but it is what we know—and *all* we know—and we respect the desert because it can be cruel and unforgiving."

There's something innate in the human spirit that knows what's difficult and what's easy, but the Arab people are to be admired. They make it through a *real* desert period, and they give honor to Allah for giving them abundance when they have it, and when they don't, they forge on anyway.

You can't tell me that the peasant doesn't know he has it hard or the pioneer woman didn't know her life wasn't easy. The desert period in our culture can be outside as well as inside, but again, it's what we make of or learn from it. It goes along with that ancient expression: "I cried because I didn't have shoes until I saw a man who didn't have any feet."

How Can This Tenet Help You?

Whereas the previous tenets have been action-oriented, it may seem that this one suggests you stay steady or seemingly quiet, but look deeper. . . . To hold steady means to stay firm in your convictions and be witness to your beliefs. *Faith* is a harsh word because you have to go on supposition. If you hold on to your beliefs in a loving God, you'll find that your faith turns into an unshakable knowing.

You see, there comes a time in every life that fits the ancient Asian proverb "When in doubt, do nothing." This means that you keep still inside as well as out when those desert periods hit. It will seem as if your life has come to a standstill and you can't seem to lurch out of it, but remember that it's all in the pattern of perfection. Think of this: No matter how diversified your life is, isn't it one that still has a lot of sameness to it? Mine certainly does. I travel, do readings, do Montel's show and other media, lecture, and write . . . over and over again. Sure I see my family, play with my grandchildren, and love my animals, but it's all the same for each and every one us—the survival of life!

Just to survive this hell on Earth is a tremendous accomplishment for anybody. The survival period can be boring, and I know that sometimes you feel so stressed and overdone that living ceases to have any joy. That's when you've got to change, no matter how hard that is to do. Yet please understand that survival can be quite different from the nothingness of the desert period. That's when you're really not doing that much and you don't know what to do, and it seems that the air of life has gone out of you. But remember, this is all a charted period that you can (like any period) use for good or ill.

Even though you chose your chart, keep in mind that you can make all things better by how you perceive them. So you hold steady and make it through with what you've learned through the desperate periods, the grief periods, and the holding (desert) periods; after all, if you stay quiet and steady, the breeze of God will come in and move you. There's always another day, a telephone call, a new friend, and episodes that will change your life to joy.

Sure, you can take the path of least resistance, but that doesn't get you anywhere except to the cardinal sins that we hear so much about. I think they should be listed as *apathy, self-indulgence,* and *spiritual bankruptcy.* Yet these aren't so much sins as roadblocks. To have apathy is deadly because there's no feeling or sympathy (Lord knows I'd rather be empathetic than have no feeling). Many times apathy is the armor we wear so that we won't be hurt, but then we feel no joy *or* pain—it's truly the "nothingness" of mere blind existence. We could learn from the love and unconditional loyalty animals give without asking for anything in return.

Self-indulgence is a case of "It's all for me, not for you" . . . what a lonely life that must be. Everything to these poor souls revolves around them and what makes them feel good. Spiritual bankruptcy is also sad because it encompasses the ones who've given up, or those conditioned to believe that a good God doesn't make bad things happen, so they choose to ignore it all. The emptiness that fills these souls must be very dark and depressing. God is *always* there for you to just lift one little finger of hope or a "maybe" of realization to let the floodgates of grace and knowledge come in.

Note that some desert periods are short, while others are long, but everyone gets them. I'd advise that instead of looking at them as negative times, look at them as if you're a marathon runner: The race can be boring, but you're strengthening your soul. So use this desert period to take stock and learn and be like the wind chimes—God's "wind" will move you to joy at what you've learned.

* * * * * *

TENET VII

Know that each life is a path winding toward perfection. It is the step after step that is hard, not the whole of the journey.

We're supposed to modify our charts without changing the ultimate learning process. Now, while they give us an overall map of life, there are many ways to get to, let's say, Miami. We can take a bus, train, car, or plane (or we can just walk or crawl if need be), but the outcome is the same: We get there and, hopefully, arrive better off than we were before we started.

Of course, if we expected life to be fair and just, then we shouldn't have come here. I'm reminded of a rock climber I once read for. He'd scaled El Capitan, a sheer cliff in Yosemite National Park, and said, "It looked great from below. Yeah, I knew it would be difficult, but I was fit for it and had been training and practicing for a year. Halfway to the top, I wanted to give up because it was so hard, but I kept going—cursing myself the whole time as I did." So it is with life. We look at our proposed chart and say, "No problem,

I can handle that!" Then we get into it and wonder what in the world we were thinking. Nevertheless, we forge ahead and hopefully are better for it.

If we look at our life in one fell swoop, it can be very daunting. As I've said so many times (and I'm not trying to be negative), life isn't too short—it's too long. Like you, in the 69 years I've lived I feel that I've actually endured many lifetimes. Even in childhood, we take steps on many paths depending on our themes and charts. Yet to look at our lives as a series of small steps can make things seem easier, for we can then analyze how we've gotten where we are now. I'm going to show you what I mean by using the example of my own life. (Those of you who have read *Adventures of a Psychic* may find some of this familiar, but it bears repeating here, so stick with me.)

The tiny steps of our childhood can be looked at (for better or worse) as the first ones on our journey of learning. My early life was fraught with an absentee and critical mother. Maybe you had a miserable father, were raised in a foster home, or were even fortunate enough to have a great home life (congratulations—few do). Even if the outward scenario is all right, sometimes we don't feel good about ourselves internally when we're very young. Either way, it's one of the steps of the journey that we can't see at the time, but which helps form who we're going to become.

The next steps are the beginnings of our schooling and levels of social interaction. Our younger years are more formative than we realize—here we begin to forge our own self-image along with the way others make us feel. Unlike my sister, I couldn't wait to get out and mingle with people. Sharon, unfortunately, was under my mother's neurotic wing and was therefore programmed to be frail, so she hid inside. This isn't meant to be critical—it's just a fact of our charts, along with the way brainwashing and apathy can work on us.

We then get into young adulthood and hopefully finish our schooling or get a job. Every part of these phases, as you know, contains both dark and light. For instance, my high school years were good, but my college years were just golden. I went to the College of St. Teresa (now known as Avila University) in Kansas City, Missouri. I had friends and parties and loved my classes. I remember when I was in the annual College Day parade as the "mad scientist." Each float had a subject, some serious and some funny (I always chose to be on a funny one—the year before I'd been a cave-woman). I had my hair sprayed white and sticking out in all directions, wore kooky glasses and a white lab coat, and I'd pasted a false eye to my cheek.

As I passed the gaggle of nuns that had gathered to watch, Sister Marcella Marie walked up to the float and asked, "Sylvia, why do you always make yourself so ugly when you're so pretty?"

I was shocked by this because my mother had always announced that "Sharon is the pretty one, but oh well . . . Sylvia *does* have somewhat of a personality." I'd never had much of a sense of my outer self (which I attribute to my grandmother), but to hear from a nun that I was pretty was mind-boggling. Later as I was telling my best friend how surprised I was, she just looked at me and said, "We thought you must know. I mean, you have a mirror don't you?" Now, this has nothing to do with my level of attractiveness, it's just an example of how we can be programmed by the reflection of others.

Anyway, back to college. My time was filled with learning, which I dearly loved. I was studying to be a teacher (in those days, girls became nurses, secretaries, or teachers—everything else was unacceptable). I took theology courses along with my education classes because I couldn't reconcile what I was taught with an all-loving God.

I used to throw these legendary parties every Saturday night with my father's consent (because it kept me home), and it was at one of these that I met Ski. Francine had said that this would be one of my biggest steps to date. I fell madly in love with him, and I interpreted Francine's message to mean that we'd be married, have children, and enjoy love everlasting.

Looking back now, I can see that I measured every male I met afterward with how I felt about Ski. He was educated and loved poetry, was fun and kind, and was like no one I'd met before—after all, he'd traveled the world as a sailor, and I was a simple Kansas City girl. The first time he kissed me, it was just like the movies: The world faded, and I said to myself, "So *this* is what all the poems and songs are written about!"

However, it turns out that he was married (although separated) with two kids. I found out because his wife wrote the college and named me the "other woman." I was called into Father Nadeus's office (God rest his loving soul), and as gently as he could, he gave me the news. To say that it broke my heart is an understatement.

I ended things with Ski, although how I did it or where any of the courage came from I don't know. I do remember thinking of the heartache his wife must be going through, and of those two little children. Ski professed that it was over with his wife, but I was also Catholic and couldn't marry a divorced man. Before we parted for the last time, he told me, "See that bright star on the right? When this life is over, I'll meet you on that one."

My heart was in shreds. For a while, the world went black, and everything seemed far away. Life looked ugly and dirty for a long time—I noticed trash on the streets and flowers that were dead rather than blooming—yet I went on having parties. Within a year, I married a policeman whom I can't say I loved, but he did seem to love me.

Francine has said to me often in my life that things happen for a reason, usually after something bad has taken place. Looking back, as much of a rebound as this marriage seemed to be, I never would have my sons and would never have gotten to California if it had not taken place. So as you can see, sometimes these crazy and seemingly unpredictable steps lead us onto the path we should be on.

My husband, Gary, had lost his job over mysterious circumstances. When a friend told him of a good offer in Sunnyvale, California, we decided to move. Consequently, I had to leave my hometown, my family, and all my friends and go to a strange place. Even though I had a job waiting for me as a teacher, I was very frightened and feeling alone— my baby, Paul, was my only comfort. I was 27 and had just recovered from a severe operation in which I'd almost died, and I was even afraid to leave the doctor who'd seen me through the whole ordeal.

In 1964, with $2,000 and a 1958 Chevrolet Impala convertible holding only what we could fit into it (which wasn't much), Gary, Paul, and I moved west. I tried to tell myself that it was an adventure, but I was so very homesick. We rented a house filled with earwigs, and that first night, I sat there on the floor with a blanket over Paul and me as the bugs dropped from a recently painted ceiling around us like rain. "I'll pretend I'm in a rain forest," I kept telling myself. It turns out that my husband's "great opportunity" turned out to be like so much smoke, so he spent the next several months halfheartedly looking for a job.

About a month after we'd arrived, my father, mother, and Sharon drove up and said, "Surprise! We've sold our house and have come to stay with you!" My father, bless his heart, wanted to be with his eldest daughter. "Besides," he said, "I hate the winters." He'd been a vice president in a large firm back in Kansas City, but he'd quit that lucrative job. For months I was the only one working, teaching at St. Albert the Great making $275 a month. Daddy did get a job selling cars, while my mother went into substitute teaching—and Gary finally became a security guard. Regardless of how much you love your folks, two families in one house is hard, but here again you learn patience and tolerance.

Although it was hell at times, being married to Gary made me grow in ways I never believed possible. Being raised with a strong father, I always felt that you did everything for the man and your life would be happy. I guess for the right person it might or should be reciprocated, but not so in my case. Perhaps if I hadn't been raised the way I was, I could have stood up for myself, but the steps of survival are truly marvelous. . . .

One day I told myself that I'd had enough. I didn't want my children (especially *male* children) to grow up and disrespect women, so I left Gary and filed for divorce. I had no money except a measly teacher's salary—although it was now up to $500 per month, even in the '70s that wasn't anything to speak of. I just couldn't go to my parents, so I moved the kids into the cheapest apartment I could find.

As I look back on my first marriage, which contained a lot of abuse and pain, there *were* good times, some laughs, the birth of our children, and even some fairly intellectual talks. So you can choose to remember the days that weren't all bad. I smile when I hear now that Gary is a born-again Christian, which I think is great as long as he stops judging everyone. When I met him in 1959, he was an atheist—how ironic life can be! Of course, I don't believe that anyone really is an atheist deep inside. I'm convinced that such people are actually driven by fear, false ego, or just plain fatalism.

Anyway, I'd known at the beginning that it was wrong to marry Gary, as my best pal of 61 years, Mary Margaret, will tell you. Nevertheless, I felt driven and compelled to do so—which was probably in my chart. We come into life with a road map, a chart we wrote to learn by. But life can be a false seductress, and sometimes we feel that we've missed out and should have followed a different path. No, the chart will have its way with us . . . just as it has with me. So we can make the best of it and enjoy the ride, or get caught up in our own doubts and fears and spend our whole life feeling as if we missed the boat. Perhaps I could have taken a less painful route to get to California . . . but I got here nonetheless. We'll always fulfill our charts, but often out of poor judgment we delay it or take the bumpy road rather than the easier one. In the long run, though, we learn. (Incidentally, Mary Margaret sends me a condolence card every April 2 because that's when Gary and I got married, and she's always said that she had guilt because she introduced us. I told her to give that up, for I was supposed to get to where I ended up.)

When I started doing readings in California, I fought it like a cornered tiger. I'd vowed after I left Kansas City that no one would know I was psychic, which certainly included my not doing readings. Sure, my friends in Missouri knew and accepted me, but there I was comfortable using my psychic abilities. Now I was going to a strange land with strange people, and I was going to keep quiet about this psychic stuff no matter what.

I remember driving up and down a boulevard in the San Francisco area and having Francine tell me that I couldn't and wouldn't stop. In fact, I'd eventually be interviewed on TV by a blonde woman, and my career would start publicly—it wouldn't be just for friends in school or women's groups like it was in Kansas City. I remember beating my hands on the steering wheel crying, "No, I won't!" Sharon was with me at the time, and I asked her, "I don't have to if I don't want to . . . do I?"

"Of course not," she said, and we both went silent, knowing that my destiny was set as surely as the road we were on.

* * *

I started taking night-school classes to get my master's degree, and that's where I met Bob Williams, a professor who was to become one of my dearest friends. We immediately hit it off and became very close. Since Bob was my teacher, we talked about literature a lot, but eventually I confided in him about my psychic abilities. He wanted me to use my talent, but I remained adamant about keeping it quiet. I was just into my second semester of his class and we were studying George Eliot's *Daniel Deronda*—particularly a part in the novel about spiritualism—when Bob suddenly announced to the entire class, "Next week Sylvia will show the class what true spiritualism is about by doing readings."

I had visions of how I was going to strangle him. But because I loved him so much, I finally consoled myself with the thought, *So what . . . it's only 40 people in the class—how far can that go?*

The next week I very nervously got up and went through my explanation of how I was born this way. Then I began to tell the students about their lives, and the ensuing uproar almost turned chaotic. During a break, I went to a small coffee bar on campus, and to my surprise, almost everyone from class was lined up for a reading. I just wanted to have a cup of coffee, but ended up answering more than 100 questions. As fate would have it, one of the women in the class was the head of a local woman's group, and she asked if I'd come and talk. I declined, she persisted, and I finally gave in. (Oh, what fools we are when we try to deceive ourselves!) I did a talk for that group and then another, and on and on it went. . . .

After I divorced Gary and remarried, my new husband, Dal, encouraged me to go public and start a foundation. I was still teaching and doing readings for the nuns and priests, and my popularity grew by word of mouth. By the end of 1972, I'd begun to do readings for five dollars and have small group lectures in our apartment. I was still teaching school as well and lived with Dal, my two boys, and Mary in a small two-bedroom apartment in a poorer part of town.

Bob had gone to Australia, where he died, leaving a huge hole in my heart. So, because he was so instrumental in my going public, I started a foundation in his honor. It was first called the Nirvana Foundation for Psychic Research, and along with readings and hypnosis, we researched everything related to the paranormal. Thank God, because so much material in my books has come from more than 30 years of research by the foundation and subsequent organizations.

It got to be too much in our small apartment, so we

moved into a townhouse. Soon after, my clientele became too disruptive for that home, too, so we found a tiny two-room commercial venue in Campbell, California. It was in the back of a building, so we didn't even have a front entrance with a sign. We had an old couch in one room that had lost its legs and was supported by bricks—this was the hypnosis room and waiting area. I was in the other room, which was like a closet with no windows. I was so claustrophobic that I hung a curtain rod with drapes on a blank wall. Many people just stared at me when they tried to look out, but it helped alleviate my closed-in feeling.

People seemed to find me. It was like the movie *Field of Dreams:* "If you build it, they will come"—and come they did. My dad worked with me at first; then, as business grew and more assistance was needed, I was fortunate to get volunteer help from some of the attendees of my study groups (which I still held in my home). The first were Larry, Laurie, and Pam and Gene Meyer (a married couple who are still with me today).

I was called by a producer from KPIX, the local CBS affiliate in San Francisco, and was asked to appear on a local television show called *People Are Talking.* It was hosted by Ann Frasier, a petite blonde (Francine scores again) with a marvelous and bubbly personality whom I'm still friends with to this day. She was later joined by Ross McGowan, a local host and personality and also a dear friend, and I spent the next ten years or so appearing frequently on their program. I made so many friends from that show, such as Bob George, Ann Miller, Steve Ober, and others—that they spread out and produced their own shows and then remembered me and gave boosts to my career later on.

How Can This Tenet Help You?

As you can see, each step of my life may not have seemed like much at the time, but when you put the entire journey together, it's not too shabby. The same holds true for *your* life's path. As I tell my clients, things can change in a second. Each step helps us to move forward and survive pitfalls—even the loves lost, the divorces, the deaths, and the illnesses. But no one can convince me that life is one long, agonizing, painful journey unless a particular individual chooses to put rocks in their own shoes.

The whole of the journey is the legacy we leave behind. After all, when I started so many years ago, they didn't know whether to bless me or burn me, but if your motive is truly to purely help and you're sincere in your soul, people will see it.

Look at the entirety of your life—not just the cracks and flaws, but each step you've taken. Of course you have your themes and your blocks to overcome—even if you try to hide from them, they'll circle around until you face them and scale that mountain of self. Now it's one thing to plod along a dusty old road as you fulfill your destiny, and it's another to be on a superhighway that goes along with speed *and* ease. So try, if you can, to find a road that has rest stops, eating places, and nice hotels—in other words, one in which God is present—it will still get you to the same place, but it will be much more comfortable.

Also, keep in mind that you've had many lives, and in each one you've learned a different facet of yourself. I've never talked much about my lives, but I'll cover a few here to show you how they build on each other.

I had a life in Kenya, which is probably why I love that country so much. I carried water, cooked for the tribe, and died early. I had a life in Austria where I wanted children but couldn't have them, and my husband left me. I had a life as an empress in Asia in which I lasted 27 days before I was poisoned. I had a life as a wife of a Crusader; he died, and I went on to teach Gnosis. There are 54 of these lives, but what comes through many of them is the will to help— in the lives that I didn't assist others, I wasn't happy. I've seemed (as we all have) to have taken steps to be better:

I've fallen and gotten up, just as you have at one time or another.

We can take detours, but we always live our charts and our destiny. We are what we are and what we're meant to be. We all end up taking the steps we must complete to finish our journey. It takes time, and it's quite a journey, but you're perfecting by the sheer fact that you come here to Earth in the first place.

✳ ✳ ✳ ✳ ✳

TENET VIII

*Be simple. Allow no man to judge you,
not even yourself, for you cannot judge God.*

Despite this tenet's advice, I do have a tendency to judge *people* who judge. When I was raising my children alone (that was in the days when most women didn't work), for example, I was told that they were going to grow up lopsided because they didn't have a father figure. I didn't buy that one, but what I did do was ensure that my blessed dad was an integral part of my boys' life. I realized early on that their father wasn't the paternal type—so, wrong or right, I took on that mantle of motherhood with a vengeance.

People who have worked with me for 30-some-odd years will attest to the fact that I never bring my personal life into my work, but if my children or grandchildren are in trouble, my world comes to a halt. I've worked through my own grief and divorces, but if my loved ones are hurt, I'm there for them and that's it. I've been judged for being so involved, but I never push . . . I'm always asked. I guess my sons and I must have formed a silent pact to be like the Three Muske-teers. Do I interfere in their relationships or in the raising of their children? Never, for that's judgment.

I feel that's part of my being psychic, for I really try to refrain from forming an opinion of human behavior unless it's evil—then, of course, all bets are off. You don't hurt peo-ple out of spite and cruelty or for the sport of it and not reap what you've sown. I'm a great believer in karma—and not the insane type that never lets you breathe without wor-rying. I mean that if you perform actions with malicious intentions, it's going to come back to you in one way or another. (I talk more about this concept in Tenet XIV.)

Now, when some members of humankind first came into form, they decided that they'd go on their own track away from God—these are the misguided souls we call "dark entities." Dark entities are much like bad children whose behavior doesn't reflect that they had great parents who did everything right. I have visions of Mrs. Hitler walking around saying, "What did I do wrong?" After all, not all of history's evil figures came from horrible homes.

I'm sure that we've all had run-ins with these dark souls (as I explain in my book *The Nature of Good and Evil*). There are no devils—there are just these entities from the Begin-ning that separated from God and decided to be missiles of destruction. In all fairness, they can give our souls fodder by being the opposite of them. I don't believe that a person who's abused has to become an abuser (unless it's in their chart to do so), but in God's plan, we can learn from these people. It's like "There but for the grace of God, go I." For example, in my early years I loved my mother, then I tried to love her, and then I couldn't love her. Sadly, she didn't love me or my sister or my dear father. It may seem shock-ing to say, but she was one of those misplaced dark entities who *couldn't* love. I guess I could have tried to have pity and compassion for her if she hadn't been so venomous up till the day she died.

The way you can tell a dark entity is more simple than

you might realize. At first, they come on very kind and sweet, and they seem to be everything that you've been looking for (male or female). But it doesn't take long for them to turn—no matter what happens, it's always your fault as far as they're concerned. I always say that they could stab you and then blame you for running into the knife. This may be a little excessive, but it's true. Ted Bundy and Jeffrey Dahmer didn't show remorse; neither has Scott Peterson or Charles Manson—it's always someone else's fault.

Dark entities leave destruction in their wake. They can wreak havoc on their loved ones, which they justify by their own track that only runs one way and causes devastation. They also don't have angels around them and seem to be devoid of a spirit guide. (If they do have one, the guide is also dark.)

All bets are off when it comes to judging dark entities. After all, no one who has any conscience or God-loving sense would refrain from judging Adolf Hitler or Osama bin Laden—our assessment of such individuals may actually be a means of survival—but God will ultimately have the final say as far as evil is concerned. Here again, in the perfection that is God, He/She doesn't judge the evildoers, but ultimately removes them. Just as on the Other Side, where we have our Home and live for eternity, all evildoers will ultimately be removed at the end of this reincarnation schematic that we're in now. They'll be reabsorbed back into God's mass and no longer be a part of creation, thus losing their individuality. (Those of us in creation keep our individuality as one of the multiple facets of God.)

The concept that "God judges" has confused theologians for years. It's just not so, for here again that makes God humanized. You see, God allowed these entities to utilize their own free will to not only separate from Him/Her, but to also incarnate as we do on this planet. Their continued existence is allowed by God in this schematic so that we can learn by incarnating in a plane of existence that contains negativity and evil.

All religions seem to have some type of war with good against evil in their dogma, as if they were trying to describe the inequities of life—yet they're neglecting the simple fact that Earth is the hardest school there is. As my guide Francine has always said, "This planet is the insane asylum of the universe. Those who come here are the bravest and want to perfect their souls faster than they would on another planet—one that is not so inundated by every type of hate and cruelty."

Think about this: It's much more difficult to learn in a perfect environment. All of us are faced with negativity each day that we live on Earth, but from this constant barrage we learn endurance, patience, and survival. And strangely enough, we learn a great deal from these dark entities—namely, how not to be. When we observe and hear about the actions of evil every day in the news, most of us turn away from it and strive to be better. As our spirituality deepens, we even fight against evil by doing good deeds, helping others, donating to charities, and giving our time and effort to causes for good.

The eighth tenet basically says that *we* are God, because we're the genetic part of God, made by God, and we carry that spark of the Divine within us. (Granted, there are some who seem to have a larger spark than others, but it's a spark nevertheless.) So we don't have the right to judge someone who doesn't measure up to what we think our standards are. Even our Lord said, "Judge not, lest ye be judged" (which I find that some people who profess to be spiritual conveniently forget) and "You without sin cast the first stone."

It's interesting how it's only taken 2,000 years for some of humankind to feel that they can judge with only half-truths. Fortunately, it's just a portion of society that acts like they have too much time on their hands—to that end, they take up causes to persecute people of different creeds, ethnic backgrounds, sexual orientation, and what have you. People are even judged by the money they make, where they live, or what their heritage is.

Many times bigotry can actually be explained by actions from a past life. For example, a woman came to our foundation years ago who seemingly hated Asians. We found out through hypnotic regression that in a past life she'd been raped by some renegade Asian men, which had tainted her present life. Once this was consciously known and released, the woman softened her racism; today, she even has an Asian best friend.

These days, we see white women with black men where I grew up in Missouri. I remember the terrible days where if you were walking on the sidewalk and a black person approached, they had to get off the sidewalk and walk in the gutter. African Americans also couldn't drink out of the same water fountains, use the same public restrooms, or eat in the same restaurants as white people, and they were forced to sit at the back of the bus. My grandmother voiced her feelings on this to anyone who would listen, but in those days it was like whistling in the wind.

At least now we can see people of color with a white person without fear of the lynching posse. Yet even though things are somewhat better, we're not totally there yet—not with Latinos, Middle Easterners, Jews, and gays, among others, still being targeted for discrimination. I guess I'll just never understand. . . . But even if you forget what bigoted issues people have, why wouldn't logic dictate that God made everyone and everything? Who do some people think they are to sit in judgment—or even propose to know the omnipotence of God—of a person's creed, sexuality, or color? You can never attain true spirituality when you have bigotry in any form in your heart.

With judging also comes hate and violence, so it has a long tail like a serpent that can recoil and turn on you. I cannot understand how, for instance, some so-called Christians can preach about Jesus and then turn around and evaluate others to the point of creating hatred and dissent among humankind. They use the parts of the Bible that are fearful in nature, which have nothing to do with Christ's teachings of love and tolerance, and call themselves "Christians." They slam other religions and even churches within the same faith, lambasting Catholics or other Protestant sects; they condemn homosexuality, mixed marriages, certain ethnic groups, and the list goes on and on. How on earth is this Christian? Jesus taught us to love one another, be tolerant and peaceful toward others, and to help one another.

It's fine for these people to be intolerant if they must, but they should at least be honest about it and not put up the sham of being kind people who love all of humanity. We've seen several instances where a religious figure in the public eye has been hurt or brought down by that "serpent of judging," and their hypocrisy was there for all to see.

In fact, it's well known that Christianity, which was based on a messiah who preached love and kindness, is one of the most intolerant religions on the face of this planet. The many wars started in the name of Jesus are proof of this. I've also heard many so-called Christian leaders say that unless the natives of Africa accept Jesus, they won't go to heaven (or, as they put it, "be saved"). To some of these people who have been "vaccinated by ignorance," I've said, "If you feel so strongly, then go into the bush and convert them yourself." I haven't seen any takers among these bigoted armchair or rocking-chair philosophers.

I've been to Kenya at least a dozen times, and people have asked me, "So what did you think about all the black people?" Each time, I've replied to this with complete honesty: "I didn't see any. I just saw *people*—kind, loving, and giving people." Men even walk down the roads holding hands together, and no one says anything. Kenyans all have the philosophy of living day to day: If they have a few shillings, they'll invite guests over and have a party all night, not caring that there may be nothing tomorrow. They live so much in the moment that if you put a Masai in jail, he'll give up and die because his "now" is forever. This is extreme, but wouldn't it be great if we just had some of that living in the now instead of running around judging everyone?

I don't want to pick on just the Christians, for most of them are loving and kind people, but the fanatics of any religion are becoming the bane of humankind. Extremists' viewpoints are fertile ground for dark entities to operate in, for they can then vent their hatred, bigotry, and destruction on the world under the guise of a religion or faith. Even the words *extreme* and *fanatic* suggest an unbending intolerance toward others who don't believe the way these people do. Of course, Jesus never did this.

We're all human and make mistakes, and by no means am I a saint. I've made a lot of blunders in my life and have never set myself up as a paragon of virtue. Like everyone else, I've stepped into many a pile of you know what. I've made some bad choices in husbands and friends. I can't drink to speak of because I get sick and vomit—not pleasant, but true (I really thank God for this intolerance). And I've been judged by many, as I'm sure all people in public life are.

That doesn't mean that celebrities should ever be above reproach, but to be knocked around by complete strangers who accuse you of being greedy; a fake or a charlatan who bilks people; fat, ugly, cruel, and having a voice that sounds like a man (yes, I've been accused of all these things) does affect you, no matter how spiritual you are. I know that I'm bluntly honest and forthright at times and can become impatient with some people, but I still love them. I'm constantly working on trying to be a better human being—and the more spiritual I get, the more I have to put the skids on myself as far as judging goes. I try to be the best person I can possibly be—and that's what I believe God wants for all of us.

Remember that God also allows us the tools of discernment and laws for social order; otherwise, we'd have anarchy running rampant, and innocent people would be taken advantage of by immoral scoundrels. As it is, new victims are enveloped by evil every day with wars, acts of terrorism, and genocide; not to mention the individual or group acts of murder, rape, child abuse, bigotry, and so on. Yet don't you find it somewhat amazing that the symbol for justice in front of most courthouses is a statue of a woman with scales (that, by the way, is the symbol for the astrological sign of Libra, which I am) in her hand—but she's blindfolded? Does this mean that justice is blind or doesn't choose to see, or that if she did see she couldn't stand what she saw?

In all seriousness, it seems that we don't want to see justice these days—not in small enclaves of society or larger scenarios that play out in the media. We see the perpetrators of crime sometimes being brought to justice, while other times we see criminals go free over some technicality. But know that, even if we don't see it, God's justice *always* comes into play. Look at Jeffrey Dahmer, who was murdered in prison—I'll never say that I wish anyone harm, but it's the way the Divine system operates.

Unfortunately, I don't think that anyone gets justice or closure in situations like this. Yes, the perpetrator may be caught and punished, but the family is still left with the loss. The only real comfort here is that, like I've said, this is a transient place—like a play, we act out our parts, then exit stage right and go Home to God.

Regardless of all the negativity I've listed in this section, I haven't meant to elicit fear but to just show you that all of us chose to come to this planet to learn faster than we would anywhere else. We only have one way to go about being happy, and that is to know that we're doing our part for peace—both out in the world and within ourselves. Please realize that we did pick this for our own perfection. After all, for the greatest education, you go to the most demanding college . . . or in this case, life on this planet.

How Can This Tenet Help You?

I've found that judging yourself can often be the worst thing you can do. (I cover some of this in my book *Sylvia Browne's Lessons for Life,* but I'd like to address it from another area here.) You learn to "judge" from your environment, even from your religious instruction that many times also teaches guilt. Nine times out of ten you've been taught that you're "bad" or did bad things, and then the conclusive result is guilt. Now you have a triple whammy—judging yourself, believing that others are doing the same, and feeling that God is, too. This tenet says to lighten up on yourself! Don't be overly concerned with judgment, because if you live the best you can and try not to hurt others, you'll be fine, especially in the eyes of God.

Now I must confess that I come down pretty hard when I see myself on TV (not the content, because I know that doesn't come from me, but my mannerisms). Once Angelia and I were sitting in my front room when I came on *Montel.* Angelia was watching, and I was trying to do some needlepoint. Out of the blue she asked, "Bagdah, why don't you keep your hands still?"

"I know," I replied. "It's either a nervous habit or I'm concentrating and don't know what I'm doing." Even so, I've got to let things like this go. I'm working on it.

It's also easy to judge situations. For example, while I'm writing this I'm in Hawaii, because my son sometimes brings me here. The first day he wanted to take me deep-sea fishing. *Damn,* I thought, *I'm going to hate this.* It wasn't because of the water, which I love—I didn't want to take time away from my writing, nor did I relish getting seasick. I went, certain of how bad it was going to be . . . and ended up having a great time.

The judgment of society can be really tough (boy, do I know!). If you keep time to a different drummer, putting forth new ideas and concepts, many times society will try to put you down. Look at the scientists who were called crazy, such as Thomas Edison. He was constantly laughed at, yet he never gave up—and, of course, he turned out to be one of the greatest inventors of all time.

Edgar Cayce was tried in a New York court for practicing medicine without a license. He won, but the headlines read

"Seer Gets Seared"—what an awful humiliation for someone who was only trying to do good. And how about our Lord, who preached love and right behavior and was then crucified for it? It can seem that people who come up with goodness, love, and truth can be judged along with the criminal . . . sometimes harsher. Nevertheless, keep in mind that you're definitely a part of the Divine, so don't let anyone judge you. And more important, get rid of your so-called demons of self-deprivation because when you do so you're defiling your own temple made for God by God.

Also, remember that bad entities never judge themselves and are impervious to any criticism—in fact, they think they're perfect. So if you ever worry about being on track, you are. It's easy to do so: Just simply ask God every day to help you and love others, and you're fulfilling your programmed chart for God. In addition, there's a difference between justifiable anger and judgment without any knowledge, research, logic, or just common sense. Sometimes your judgment fails, but if you listen to that inner voice (not some preconceived notion), you'll become more psychic.

Life has holes in it, so fill them up. Worrying about your appearance wastes time, so if you don't have the looks you want, concentrate on the "inner" you. And don't listen to others' judgments—after all, at the final tally it's just you and God. As Jesus said in Matthew 5:45: "That you may be sons of your Father in heaven: for He makes His sun rise on the evil and on the good, and sends rain on the just and the unjust." So you see that to God, all are equal. That doesn't mean the unjust won't get theirs; it simply means that you can't judge except for evil. And when you *do* judge evil, be careful, because you don't know the path these people have chosen. It really boils down to this: *When in doubt, don't judge at all.*

* * * * * *

TENET IX

You are a light in a lonely, dark desert who enlightens many.

All right . . . it's time to take a long, hard look at the world we live in. Most enlightened messengers have recognized that this planet we inhabit in a physical body is not just a desert, but it's also a place of illusion and many times *de*lusion.

For example, in *The Teaching of Buddha,* Bukkyo Dendo Kyokai states: "To adhere to a thing because of its form is the source of delusion. If the form is not grasped and adhered to, this false imagination and absurd delusion will not occur. Enlightenment is seeing the truth and being free from such a foolish delusion."

He also says that "since everything in this world is brought about by causes and conditions, there can be no fundamental distinctions among things. The apparent distinctions exist because of people's absurd and discriminating thoughts. In the sky there is no distinction of east and west; people create the distinctions out of their own minds and then believe them to be true."

So once we understand and embrace the world for what it is—and realize that the oasis for this desert resides on the Other Side—all of life becomes easier (especially when we realize that this planet is a learning plane that contains evil and negativity). T. S. Eliot wrote about the "wasteland," and I don't want to belabor the point and seem overly negative, but this world *is* a wasteland. In all fairness, it's also a place of beauty, joy, goodness, and even propriety. There are people to love, families to be close to, and an abundance of kindness to share. Look at Martin Luther King, Jr., or Mother Teresa, both of whom tried to make this world a better place with a dream: One had a vision of an ecumenical world where everyone would love each other regardless of color; while the other aspired to save the poor from sickness and dying.

We should also keep in mind that this world is what we make it. While we're here, why not light our lamp of enlightenment? When we do, we find that we inspire and attract others.

Someone asked me just the other day, "What if I love and I'm hurt?" Well, Tennyson said it better than anyone with this: "'Tis better to have loved and lost than never to have loved at all." In other words, loving and giving a person a light in their soul actually makes *our* souls deeper and fuller. Even if it doesn't work out, then we'll go on to love again and light another soul—provided that we don't become callous and close ourselves off and never feel again. If we do that, then we only end up hurting ourselves . . . along with the countless others who would have loved us back.

I've loved and lost (and gained), but I've always recognized that spiritually I can't live in a desert of my own making. Now you may prefer to platonically love children or animals or friends (or God)—no matter, you're putting out a light from your soul. I've heard people wonder, "Why should I help anyone? I mean, what have they done for me?" Well, probably nothing. After all, the type of person who would say such a thing hasn't taken the time to love; consequently, not many will love them back. Their only existence is themselves, and that's all they care about. I know *you* don't want to be this type of person!

When we make baskets for the poor, do we need to know each family that a toy or turkey was given to? Of course not—we just send it out! So should light and love be packaged up and sent wherever it needs to go. Love is the water on a dry desert that enables the flowers of joy to grow.

Los Angeles is a desert, yet look at how the foliage has grown up and made the area lush. So does the love we send out to others: It may not hit the mark it was intended for, but it will hit *some* mark, somewhere, sometime—and even if *you* don't know it, God does. It's also written in gold in the Hall of Records (this is where the phylum of angels known as the Dominions record our deeds in our charts), and a light will go on in someone's lonely desert of a soul because of this good deed or action.

* * *

I'd like you to remember one very important thing: Don't leave *yourself* in a desert or forget to light your own candle, because if you don't have a light, you can't spark anyone else's. Our Lord even makes it very clear that you should never hide your light under a bushel. In other words, bring it out into the open! Each time you love and give to others, you give water to the desert of your own soul, which may need compassion, love, advice, or sympathy just as much as—or more than—the people you're helping.

When I think of lights in a desert, I automatically think of Grandma Ada. She was so self-sufficient, yet her light inspired everyone around her. For example, when she was 81, there was a large broken branch on a tree that was threatening to fall on her tomatoes (this was when she lived in a little cottage, before she was relegated to the flophouse). My boyfriend at the time was going to get on a ladder and saw the branch off. She looked up and said, "That's ridiculous," and with one hand reached up and ripped it off. Much later, we'd laugh about this, and he'd say, "Never let me get into a fight with your grandmother!"

Then when Grandma Ada was 84 she broke her hip (which, as you probably know, can be deadly for the elderly). She went to the hospital, where they put her in a cast and placed her in a bed. As soon as all the medical personnel had left her alone, she promptly got up, got dressed, hobbled out the door, got a cab, and went home. I got the call from the doctor who was frantic that they'd lost Ada Coil. For a moment I was concerned, but then I realized exactly what she'd done and where she was.

I went over to her little house, and there she was: cleaning and fixing dinner for Brother. I asked her why she left, since she had everyone at the hospital worried sick. She looked at me with surprise and said, "Well, I just felt that they'd done all they could do for me, so I left. Besides, who would take care of Brother?" She recovered just fine, and when asked about her hip, she'd wave it off as just a foolish mistake, and that was the end of it. Talk about your lights in the desert! She truly was the one that my entire family looked up to.

How many times have we heard that a parent dies and the entire family falls apart? Unfortunately, it's because that person was holding the only light, and the rest circled around it like moths to a flame. When that person dies, no one else knows how to carry the torch, so to speak. Sometimes it's easier to let someone else carry the light, but if you never pick it up, you'll never know what you're missing. To be the torchbearer that sparks other people's lights is really the bottom line of what life is about. We all contribute to making this world what it is, so let's all make a concerted effort to be a light and make the world a brighter and more loving one.

If you're having trouble finding your own light, try the

meditation below. It will take you through a long, lonely desert and then into a beautiful meadow.

You are in an arid desert, and your feelings of loneliness and even isolation are rising to the surface. Soon, even as tired as you are, you come to the top of a sandy hill, and below you see a beautiful meadow with grass and flowers. The colors are so bright that you can barely stand to look at the scene at first.

With a renewed energy, you run down the hill and into the meadow. When you arrive, you begin to see loved ones who have passed gathering around you. (Even your pets are there!) All of a sudden, a pillar of light descends—seeming to come right through the top of your head—and spreads through your entire body. You immediately feel refreshed and realize that without the desert of life, you would never be able to enjoy the light of your own spirituality.

During this relaxation period, think of yourself as a giant pop-it bead of gold who's pushing your individual energy of love to the person or fellow bead on your right. (When several people have done this in my presence, I've seen the whole room light up with a golden light that then forms a giant pyramid.) Then send this love and energy out to anyone who needs it. Maybe someone in a dark alley will get a bit of your golden light and never know who sent it. Or perhaps a sick or dying person will have their suffering lifted, or someone on drugs will become enlightened.

Haven't you ever heard somebody say, "One day the pain just went away," "For some unknown reason I just decided to stop drinking," or "I got tired of feeling sorry for myself and went out and began to help others"? How do you know where this remote healing goes? It doesn't matter, nor should it—it will go through the desert. Maybe you won't know until you reach the Other Side where it went, but know that it will go where it's needed.

How Can This Tenet Help You?

Tenet IX seems to mirror some of the others, but when you look at it more deeply, you'll see that it's referring to the personal you—that is, the essence of who you are.

Now, how can you become a light? I asked myself this when I was very young and started out really wanting to save the world (not ostentatiously, but to bring about some sort of order and peace). Even in my writings or lectures, the amount of people I reach is small compared to the world, but I began to realize that if you can light just one candle, that candle will spark another and another. That's where you come in, for if I can light your candle, then I know that you'll illuminate another candle and another, and then you'll become a light yourself (if you're not already one).

When I started my readings and lectures in my home, I often wondered where my light would go—but I kept telling myself to just keep going one step at a time and see what happened. I decided to hone it down to what I wanted to get across against all odds. After sifting through many things, I was led to the logical conclusion that we have an all-loving Father and Mother God, and we live many lives to perfect and follow Christ's teachings. Was it easy? Hell no! I was bucking years of political and religious dogma, but I kept telling myself what my professor Bob Williams always said: "They can hurt your feelings, but they can't eat you."

To that end, know that you're going to question yourself during this process, and even on a few dark nights you'll wonder why you're doing what you're doing, but that's the dark side trying to attack you and make you despair. When this happens, just "eject that tape" and shine that light of yours that gives solace to others, a shoulder to cry on, or someone to listen or sit with in times of grief. Even helping people pass over is a blessed thing to do.

Whatever you do, in whatever manner you do it, do it with love. Is it hard? Sure it is! I mean, do you think that every morning I get up dancing and singing? Some days are tiring and others are gut-wrenching, but overall, the key is that I love what I do. I wouldn't want to do anything else but be with you and around you and talk to you. That's my love affair.

And let's face it: If we humans don't get it right this time (I feel that we only have 100 years or so left on this planet), maybe it will never get done. We have to learn to get over ourselves and help others as Jesus taught—after all, he wouldn't have said to love your neighbor as yourself just to be saying it. All the "messengers" such as Buddha, Christ, and Mohammed taught the same thing, and all of their work will be for nothing if we all don't "get it," and even more important, "practice it."

It's just like the cross: Pieces of it are religious relics and a substantiation of many people's faith. Most of us, however, carry our faith inside our heart. Yes, I wear a cross, but it's because of what I feel it represents for me. We love God in our own way—when we do so, we don't have to keep obsessing about our so-called ego. After all, *ego* only means "the I am." And when you get down to it, who I am and what I've accomplished through life after life simply comes down to loving others. This is where the light for each and every one of us comes from. We must never forget this.

✳ ✳ ✳ ✳ ✳ ✳

TENET X

Let no one convince you that you are less than a God. Do not let fear imprison your spiritual growth.

I have to tell you that when I heard first heard this tenet, it really threw me. Me, a God . . . come on! Give me a break—let's put our ego in perspective! But then as I researched, I began to see what this tenet really means. We're the true genetic offspring of our Divine Creators, just as we are of our parents and grandparents. So, in other words, if I can say that I got my philosophy and strength from my grandmother, my drive from my father, or my tenacity from my grandfather, then why can't I go further and realize that I'm part and parcel of the Divine? Nevertheless, it seems so difficult for us to accept this fact, and that's where the fear comes in.

Two emotions cannot occupy the mind at the same time, so if we're full of fear, we can't love; by the same token, if we're full of love, we can't fear or hate. While *hate* is a harsh word, I've found that people who are fearful do indeed hate being that way. They often try to change themselves to cope with (or do other things to take their mind from) their fears, but without spiritual help, it usually ends in failure—and the fears loom ever larger.

The dictionary describes *fear* as "a feeling of agitation and anxiety caused by the presence of the imminence of danger." Sometimes this can be *imagined* danger, but it doesn't matter—the adrenaline kicks in for flight or fright. Fear is a normal part of life, usually boiling down to the feeling that we're helpless and out of control. I can't tell you the times when I've told people who were afraid of flying that if they could pilot the plane themselves they'd feel better, and nine times out of ten they agree.

In this day and age, our entire society seems to feel out of control. We live with the ever-present danger of terrorism, especially after 9/11, and most of us don't feel safe. And that collective fear is a powerful emotion that seems to have tentacles like an octopus—it starts out small, but as it grows, its arms go out to many things instead of one. Take heart, though: No matter how many arms your personal concern may have, it usually goes back to one event, whether from this life or a past one.

For example, I recently spoke with a woman who had four boys. Strangely, she didn't worry about the youngest three, but with her oldest, it was getting to the point where she was obsessed with where he was every moment—she was completely convinced that she was going to lose him. Looking at her chart, I saw that she'd had four children in a past life in Poland. The family's house had caught fire, and she was able to save three of her children, but the oldest died. The woman had carried over the fear of this loss to her current life—but once she was able to face and release it, her dread disappeared.

Then there was the woman who was deathly afraid of snakes, especially cobras. Now, she lived in a brownstone in New York City, hardly the place where you'd find a cobra under the bed, but she was paralyzed by this fear nonetheless.

She was told by therapists that it was an unfounded fear and she should just get over it.

The woman scheduled a reading with me, and I picked up that in a past life an irate husband who was convinced that she'd been unfaithful had pushed her into a cave with cobras. Of course they bit her, and she died a painful death. She'd carried this fear over, and it became more acute the closer she came to the age she'd been when it had occurred. (In my research, I've found that this is not uncommon; various triggers such as age, similar incidents, and so forth can activate a fear or memory from a past life.) Once this became known to her conscious mind, the fear dissipated.

Now some may say that these are just healing stories for the mind. Well, even if they were (which they in no way, shape, or form were), if it works, who cares? The truth always connects with the subconscious, and even the best hypnotist or psychologist will tell you that you can't lie to the subconscious (or what I like to call "the super-conscious"), where all memory exists. Sometimes because of this, people just get over a fear that they had most of their life, and they never know why. It can also happen in reverse, in which a person who never had a fear of something has it suddenly come upon them out of the blue—for example, the man who was never afraid of heights until he reached the age of 26, which coincided with the exact time that he was pushed into a volcano as a sacrifice to the gods in an Aztec life.

Most of us have heard about the cases in which some idiot therapist implants a memory in his or her patient, such as, "You were molested." An implanted memory is a Band-Aid—and a fake one at that—which eventually falls off, showing the still-festering wound. However, many children have all-too-real night terrors, which are left over from past lives.

The best way to deal with this is to go into their room, hold them, and tell them that this is not happening *now*, but it's something that's coming from another time and place. I guarantee this will work. I've done it (or had my sons and daughters-in-law do it) with my grandkids, and it stops immediately. Strangely enough, I could even break my sons' fevers by going in and telling them that it would be gone and they would be well. Their systems, with God's help, would fight the illness, and in the morning they'd be running around like wild deer, wearing me out. Thank God, though—that was better than sick boys.

* * *

Sometimes fear is so strong that it can be paralyzing. The only difference between a fear and a phobia is that phobias can be more irrational—which doesn't help someone who's suffering from them. Again looking to the dictionary, a phobia is described as an "abnormal and irrational fear of a specific thing or situation that compels one to avoid it, despite the awareness and reassurance that it is not dangerous. A strong, unreasonable fear, dislike, or aversion."

The problem with these negative emotions is that they stop spiritual growth. There are some universal fears that scientists and doctors agree on, such as the fear of falling and darkness that we're supposedly born with. I never found this to be true with the children I raised, however. The universal concerns that much of society obsesses over are prodigious in length, but here are a few of them: fear of exposure, death, pain, loss, rejection, loneliness, abandonment, rape, burning, drowning, heights, crowds, outward appearances, cancer, blindness, and becoming homeless. I feel that I've heard most of them from my readers and clients—of course, as soon as I say this, I'll hear of another one.

Ancient Indian beliefs state that a snake may not kill you, but the *fear* of a snake might. How many times do we conjure up our own worries that are unfounded, only to have them gradually take over our mind? I can remember as a young girl that I heard so much about hell that I became almost sick with guilt over any little thing. Even looking at a pair of underpants hanging on a clothesline, thinking that they covered "naughty parts," would give me sweaty palms. In those days, to just think a bad thought was a sin, so guess what? We thought bad thoughts! It's like saying, "Don't think of a pink elephant." Naturally, a pink elephant is the first thing that appears in your mind.

My father, bless his heart, could see that I was suffering, so one night he came in my room to ask me what was wrong. In between spasms of tears, I managed to get out that I was thinking bad thoughts and was going to hell. "There isn't any hell, baby—it's only in our own mind," he gently said. "But go ahead and think all the bad thoughts you want, and then you'll be done with it."

Presto! Just those wise words of consent drove the so-called demons of fear away, and even at nine years of age I felt what I realize now was grace being allowed to come in.

What upsets me is that our religious beliefs tend to add to our fears instead of quieting them. We're afraid of hell or retribution by a capricious God who plays favorites. This, of course, is a powerful emotion that keeps people controlled and in line. I hate the expression "Fear God." Why should we fear not only what we're part of, but an all-loving Creator and Parent? I prefer the Sikh doctrine, which resonates with the belief that all people have the right to follow their own path to God without condemnation from others. The Gnostics believe the same thing, which is probably why Christ was of the Essene sect.

There's an old saying that goes, "Fear is a great enemy of mankind. It is the enemy of his progress. It disturbs his peace and harmony. It sucks or saps his vitality and energy. It drains the nervous system of its reserve of energy. It produces weakness." And one of my favorite sayings, "A coward dies many times before his death," says a lot, too. In other words, the brave know what they're afraid of, but cowards live in abject fear and imagine all the ways they can die. This is disabling and stunts spiritual growth.

We're all sons and daughters of God—even the dark entities who will eventually be absorbed back into His/Her uncreated mass. You may wonder, "Well, if we're so Divine, then how can we make so many mistakes?" Francine told me years ago that the human form makes us stupid. I thought, *Boy, in my case that's true—I certainly wouldn't have picked some of the people in my life that I did!* Yet later I realized, *Yes, I would. Even an evil mother teaches us how not to be. A bad marriage can teach us how to rely on ourselves. Loneliness is a state of mind. My writing is self-imposed aloneness, but it's what I enjoy.*

I'm not saying that when life gets too debilitating we shouldn't seek counseling. In extreme cases, it's even okay to take pharmaceuticals—but it's not okay to immediately rely on them because you have an anxious moment here and there, are experiencing natural fears, or are stricken by grief. When I lost nine people who were very close to me in three months, for instance, the doctor said, "Sylvia, you're depressed. I'm going to prescribe an antidepressant."

"I'm in grief," I replied, "and you don't have a pill for that."

Now that doesn't mean that those who can't pull themselves out of a hole for a reasonable amount of time (for each person it's different) shouldn't seek medical help. If you become incapacitated, then realize that God made doctors, too.

Most of us at one time or another think that we're going crazy. So many people who saw things like I do or heard things like I do used to be dubbed crazy, while people who astrally projected were locked up. I tend to feel that crazy people don't know that they are, so they don't worry about it. They think that they're normal! That doesn't mean we shouldn't be tested or see a doctor like I did, but we really must accept that there are so many things on this planet that we will never know or understand.

How Can This Tenet Help You?

The East Indian belief, which is identical to our Gnostic one, is that ignorance is the cause of fear. Sometimes I despise the word *ignorance* because it makes us feel stupid. It actually means "disregarding a truth that's available," but many times we don't even know where to go to look for the answers, so it can be like trying to find the proverbial needle in a giant haystack.

Don't mistake being nervous or anxious as not being normal. Being obligated to go to court, see a doctor, attend an important meeting, or face an ex-love—these are all normal types of situations in which you might feel trepidation. It's only when it rules your life that it becomes a problem. And don't confuse foolhardiness with lack of fear. Sensible people can take chances, but those who venture out of the realm of reason can become daredevil types who cause great danger to themselves and others. We can't always judge these kinds of people, though, as some individuals get an adrenaline rush from testing fate. I like the expression "Don't try this at home."

Of course, normal fears of losing our loved ones or having our family harmed are natural and come with a human body. Jesus' kingdom was not of this world and neither is yours, but you can't stop the grief or fear of loss—it comes with the territory. Yes, we know that our loved ones went Home and are happy, but we're stuck here missing them.

As your knowledge gained through reading, research, and working with people expands, fear does diminish. First of all, you become more Godlike and not so rooted in your own transient, mortal body. To know that you're not alone in your fears is also a great cure.

There are many moments when I experience anxiety (I pretty much stomp fear down), such as before every lecture, Montel or Larry King's shows, a pay-per-view special, and so forth—I'm not so concerned for myself, but for all the people I love. I don't want to embarrass them, and I only want to give out the right information and be a pure prophet for God.

I so clearly remember the first pay-per-view special I did: I was beside myself because Montel and my publisher, Hay House, had their money riding on me. (If it had been my own money backing the show, I would have been uneasy, but not fearful.) Anyway, I obsessed about it for a solid week. Not even Montel's kind words—"You're going to be great, girlfriend"—or anyone else's words, for that matter, helped. *What if I freeze up?* I worried. *After all, it's live!* (I won't work with a TelePrompTer or script, so I always fly by the seat of my pants.) *What if I go numb and just stare into the camera or say something stupid? Maybe I'll just break a leg, but that won't work because the time slot's already paid for.*

Of course when the time came, it worked out all right, and everyone got their investment back. I've been on TV for 30 years, but to have people put their money on me just frightened me. I worked through the fear, and the second and third pay-per-views I did were fine—but that first one was grueling.

Through our massive statistical references of past-life regressions, my ministers and I have seen cure after cure of fear-related problems. True, many problems with fear can come from this life. A fear of drowning because some dumb parent threw a child in the water and said, "Swim," thus causing a terrible fear of water, can be an example. But more times than can be counted it comes from a past life, and that's why people can't trace it in a therapy that just covers *this* life.

So, going back to my own regression, I had a life in England where I'd been given money collected by the villagers to release a prisoner. In my hectic travels, I'd lost it, and a fear of losing money resulted. This is why I was so frightened about the pay-per-view (cell memory returns in the strangest ways). So, as they say, to face your fears sometimes doesn't help, but having knowledge of where the phobic reaction comes from can, because understanding releases us from the unknown "boogie man" that hides in the closet of our minds. As this tenet says, you are nothing less than a God, and in truly believing this you can learn from your fears. You don't have to keep them, however, because they will imprison your soul so that it can't grow.

For those of you with phobias and physical maladies that don't seem to respond to medicine, you might want to try this on yourself: Ask God to take you out of that past-life groove and put you in *this* time frame—and to see that the past is gone and has nothing to do with now. You might be surprised by the results.

You can also check when your fear first started and try to meditate yourself back to a life in which it could have started. What were the circumstances that led up to it? What were you doing? What was happening or what did someone say right before the phobia or anxiety happened? Then go to a reputable therapist or certified hypnotherapist and ask God at night to take it away. It will go, your life won't be filled with the emotion of fear, and you'll get your God-center back. It's there if you find it (as I did) by reading, researching, and questioning.

An East Indian proverb says: "Imagining fears causes diseases." That is to say that fear can make you immobile and stressed and consequently can make you ill. If we truly believe that fear is illusionary or if we say that it comes from a real point of entry and then light is shined upon it, it cannot live. Another proverb says: "Courage is eternal, it will not die, but the thrusting of fear is a terror in the soul and blocks out our Godliness."

You are a God and carry that light. Like our Lord said in Matthew 7:12, "Therefore, whatever you want men to do to you, do also to them, for this is the law and the prophets." I've tried to always live by this "golden rule," and knowing this—and that we're human vehicles—it has alleviated fear from my life a great deal. Spirituality then pours in, and by going through it, your soul will have learned and be more open to grace.

✳ ✳ ✳ ✳ ✳ ✳

TENET XI

Do not allow the unfounded belief in demons to block your communion with God.

Demons haven't always been around. You see, at one time humankind didn't know how to explain the horrors or inequities of life, so they figured that a God Who had to be appeased was behind everything. Then they graduated to trying to explain the negative aspects of life by coming up with evil entities or demons.

All religious texts refer to evil. Our ancestors not only couldn't come to the logical deduction of a perfect, loving God, but they also couldn't believe that evil was nothing more than a by-product of God's creations, not God.

Several documentaries and writings on the historical life of Jesus said that during his "lost years" he visited India, Tibet, and several other countries in the Near and Middle East. (My spirit guide Francine has confirmed this, too.) It was during this time that Christ learned about other religious philosophies and practices, including healing. The "casting out of demons" phraseology that's mentioned many times in the Bible when Jesus did a healing is in fact a direct reference to the Indian belief that demons caused illnesses. Christ realized that a mostly unlearned population had to be related to in terms that they'd understand.

Take the following, for instance:

> Now when the sun was setting, all who had persons sick with various diseases brought them to him. And he laid his hands upon each of them and cured them. And devils also came forth from many, crying out and saying, "Thou art the Son of God." And he rebuked them, and did not permit them to speak, because they knew that he was the Christ. . . . (Luke 4:40–41)

> And it came to pass, while he was in one of the towns, that, behold, there was a man full of leprosy. And when he saw Jesus he fell on his face and besought him, saying, "Lord, if thou wilt, thou canst make me clean." And stretching forth his hand he touched him, saying, "I will; be thou made clean." And immediately the leprosy left him. And he charged him to tell no man, but, "Go, show thyself to the priest, and offer the gift for thy purification, as Moses commanded, for a witness to them." But so much the more the tidings spread concerning him, and great crowds gathered together to hear him and to be cured of their sicknesses. But he himself was in retirement in the desert, and in prayer. (Luke 5:12–16)

Now several things or concepts are happening here. First, you don't need a long procedure to heal, since it's the laying on of hands in the name of God or our Lord that does it. Second, in all four of the Gospels (of Matthew, Mark, Luke, and John), our Lord states that when you do a good deed you don't need to have it told to everyone—it really is between you and God. If you did get all your rewards here, then what lesson would you have learned?

Next, when the "devil" was trying to seduce Jesus in the

desert, through logic and reading the text, we can see that the meaning is allegorical. The following is from Luke 4:1–13, and I've included commentary in parentheses and italics:

Then Jesus, being filled with the Holy Spirit, returned from the Jordan and was led by the Spirit into the wilderness *(How many times, just like Tenet IX says, must we go to the desert period to learn by temptation or just loneliness—or finding it in our soul not to fall into despair and negate evil or depression?)* . . . being tempted forty days by the devil. And in those days he ate nothing, and afterward, when they had ended, he was hungry. *(How many times in our darkest time do we hunger not just for food, but for enlightenment?)* And the devil said to him, "If you are the son of God, command this stone to become bread." *(It's heartening for me to read here that in the toil to bring truth, we're always going to be challenged by naysayers.)* But Jesus answered him, saying, "It is written, man shall not live by bread alone, but by every word of God." *(It's true we need sustenance for the body, but if the soul is in despair, the body will go into stress and even illness.)*

Then the devil, taking him up on a high mountain, showed him all the kingdoms of the world in a moment of time. And the devil said to him, "All this authority I will give to you, and their glory; for this has been delivered to me, and I give it to whomever I wish." *(This is interesting because our planet doesn't belong to the devil per se, but to negativity. It's ruled by hatred, prejudice, and all the other hardships we've experienced in this life or even other lives.)* "Therefore, if you will worship before me, all will be yours." *(This asks what it profits a man to gain the whole world, if he loses his soul. Now does this mean that we can't enjoy comfort and some luxury in life? Of course not, but if you're bound by the evils of the world and use it for your own gain or fame, you're headed for spiritual bankruptcy.)*

And Jesus answered and said to him, "Get behind me, Satan! For it is written, you shall worship the Lord your

God, and him only you shall serve." Then he brought him to Jerusalem, set him on the pinnacle of the temple, and said to him, "If you are the Son of God, throw yourself down from here. For it is written: 'He shall give His angels charge over you, to keep you,' and 'In their hands they shall bear you up, lest you dash your foot against a stone.'" And Jesus answered and said to him, "It has been said, 'You shall not tempt the Lord your God.'"

Now when the devil had ended every temptation, he departed from him until an opportune time.

So we can see that this is an analogy of life and its trials and temptations. The main principle here isn't the devil at all—instead, the story points to what life throws at us and what the outcome will be if we lend our life, our soul, or even our name or power to evil. We'll become miserable, because I believe that in good souls there's an innate guardianship that screams "No!" when things are tainted. All that glitters is not gold, so look at the devils or demons as a type of ancient litany constructed by human beings to understand the hell of this planet.

Like Jesus, Buddha also used demons as metaphors for evil in order to communicate to the uneducated masses. If you've read as many religious texts as I have, you'll swiftly come to the conclusion that the so-called demon is only a ruse. Yet the fear of hell or the devil has literally built many ornate edifices. Not that I don't think we should honor God, but I wonder why people don't realize that God exists everywhere. Don't get me wrong; I love to go into temples and churches (when I'm in New York, I love to visit St. Patrick's Cathedral, especially when it's quiet), but we also have to remember that Buddha, Mohammed, and Christ didn't teach in such places of worship—they happened after the fact. Instead, these wise prophets went to the people of the land and delivered their messages of love and peace.

With so many messengers preaching love and right actions, why has humankind gone so far to the negative side? Well, as I've explained, they just didn't know how to explain the inequities of life, so they came up with demons and hell. Such dogma also gave early religions a way to control people with fear, which in turn gave them a lot of money to keep their religions going. (Don't you find it amazing that the fear that was utilized to control the uneducated masses of the past is still successful today with the "educated" masses? Today, many so-called religious people interpret the stories literally, which constitutes confusion because their illogical and literal interpretation also makes them lose their original meanings. This is a case of tradition and history—which, I might add, was written by the winners—overcoming education and logic. How tragic.)

Humankind has a primordial fear of the unknown, so when bad things keep happening, it seems that we slip back into an ancient belief that's in our DNA, which says that there has to be some outside force responsible, such as a devil. I find it funny that we've spent so much time on worrying and talking about the devil that this concept has become stronger and larger than God. If we adhere to a good life and avoid evil, why do we have to dwell on all the negative? If we're continually worried about demons, we've not only negated a loving, merciful God, but we'll become so preoccupied with fear that it takes over our thoughts and minds. Consequently, love, harmony, and peace—along with the communion with God—are blocked here, which begets ego and self-importance.

Human beings who have separated from God out of their own ego and then took on a chart or direction of destruction can also render good people impotent. They do so by using us and playing on our weaknesses; by hurting, rejecting, and abandoning us; and by coming in a very seductive face and utilizing charm and other means to suck us in. Yet such dark entities know that they can't possess us, for there's a primary link between God and ourselves that won't allow it. If a spirit guide can't read our minds or force us to do something, then why would a lower form of entity be able to take hold of our life, actions, and mind?

The courts don't even buy this "devil made me do it" type of syndrome. Ronald DeFeo, Jr., the young man who killed his family several years ago, tried that absurd defense after "the Amityville horror" occurred. He even had two so-called paranormal investigators trying to come to his defense. It didn't work, thank God. Can you imagine? With all the injustices we see, all we need is everyone who commits a horrendous act claiming that the devil made him do it. (Of course, this doesn't apply to the truly mentally deranged.)

Another fallacy is that in some cultures, people who go crazy are thought to be possessed. This is actual ignorance because these societies are uneducated about illness, heredity, post-traumatic stress disorder, mental breakdowns, and so forth, all of which can lead to real forms of mental illness. In other words, the mind is just an organ that can be affected—or infected—the same as any other organ.

And as I've said so many times, there's no such thing as an evil ghost either. Such entities are confused and sometimes deranged, but they're mainly just aggravated that you're in their territory. You can usually release them by telling them that they're dead and they need to go to the brilliant white light. (It can also be helpful to use holy water and a crucifix in every room, open up your home, and surround it with salt.) I know that some of these spirits can be tenacious—I've personally encountered a few who won't listen, so you either have to move or put up with it. But know that they'll eventually be picked up by someone from the Other Side who will convince them that they need to come Home.

Finally, at least once a week I hear that someone put a curse on a person's family. This is ridiculous . . . but not to the person going through it. If anyone would have a curse on them, it would be me. All of the charlatans I've turned in or called and then reported to the authorities would have hundreds of Sylvia dolls out there full of pins. But the only way "black magic" works is because certain cultures have been conditioned by years of belief. Remember that the mind is a powerful mechanism, which can be the healer of your body or the faculty that makes you sick. I have great respect for Vodun (also known as Voodoo), the true religion that has its roots in Africa *and* Catholicism, and their own ancestral gods that protect them from evil, but you always find the renegades in any religion. Satanic cults, on the other hand, practice no true religion; instead, they contain the dregs of the earth, which have no spirituality and merely want the thrill of flirting with the rituals (and sex) that accompany such endeavors.

How Can This Tenet Help You?

I'm sure you've figured out by now that *there is no devil*—there is only humankind's construction of evil, and the devil is its figurehead, so to speak. It was devised out of ignorance to explain the inequities of life on this hellhole of a planet.

Nevertheless, even in this day and age I still hear from people on practically a daily basis who feel that they've been cursed or tortured by the devil. In the first place, if there was such a creature, what makes you or me so important that he'd bother with us? Wouldn't he go after Billy Graham or someone else who's important and doing God's work? The whole concept of a devil is just not true.

A woman once told me that she thought getting old was evil. I replied, "No, but you can hate it enough to fight it all the way down to your heels." People are afraid to use the word *hate,* and I don't know why. After all, I hate hunger and strife, and I hate child abuse and molestation . . . I certainly don't want to love that evil! So instead of worrying about these silly demons, fight negativity, ignorance, and bigotry by standing up for human rights, and for the needs of children and the aged. That's what will keep your communion with God alive.

The logo for Novus Spiritus connects the three circles of gratitude, loyalty, and commitment like the trinity, and then interlocks them with a dove that can be the Holy Spirit or the ancient symbol of the Mother God. I have jewelry with this logo on it, and a good portion of the proceeds from the sale of it (which is available on my Website, **www.sylvia.org**), goes to multiple-sclerosis charities. Our church also adopts children from the Christian Children's Fund, gives to a home for the elderly as well as one for children, and donates free spiritual counseling through our ministry. It's not because we're so great, but it's what we can do right now. Even so, it never seems like enough, but as we say, "It's better to light one little candle than none at all."

Sometimes the best way to battle negativity is to simply give of yourself—for instance, go out to the elderly and talk to them, which will greatly help remove their fear and loneliness. It's heartbreaking to see so many of our elders put in homes—in fact, I want to have enough money to start my own place for the aged (ideally for children, too)—but sometimes we can't physically or medically take care of them. It's worst for those who are alone every day with no one to come and visit them. In other cultures this is unheard of—they think that we Americans are uncaring and even evil for neglecting our elderly. In many cases, the problem has to do with lifestyle, because so many families now have both parents working, and they don't have the time and energy it takes to care for their elders. If you're in this type of situation, then *make* the time to visit as often as you can because it will help a great deal.

I absolutely hate getting older—not out of vanity but because the body wasn't supposed to last this long anyway. It's the bounce that goes out of the step and the funny aches and pains that go with it. I'm looking at my 70th birthday this year, and I keep hearing my grandmother's words coming back to haunt me: "Someday you'll know what it's like to be a young woman trapped in an old body." Well, dearest love of my life, I'm beginning to. In fact, I just had a physical, and the doctor said, "You're in great shape." And I added, "For the shape I'm in."

I know that God loves me—and you—unconditionally, but before I started my church I went into a slump. "Who do you think you are?" I asked myself. "You should just give it up and stay in your quiet corner of the world." As soon as I realized that I was being torn, I got rid of my fears and went straight ahead. In other words, our own emotions take over our intellect and take on any form we fear—it's got nothing to do with demons.

Such fear also points to a misplaced ego. For example, as I once asked a friend who was convinced that the devil was always torturing her, "Why are you so important that the devil would want to torture you?" After a moment she said, "You know, you could be right."

"Just get involved with others and forget about this devil," I replied.

Of course, many so-called fortune-tellers would tell my friend that her "demonic possession" could be cured for the right sum. A client once told me that she'd been told by a "psychic" to hand over her Mercedes-Benz because it was possessed. I asked her, "If it was so possessed, then why did she want it?"

I try to get the names of these individuals to turn them into the local district attorney's office, but most of the time superstition runs high and people are too afraid of being cursed to give me this information—sad but true. Before you visit *any* psychic, see who knows them, what they've done, and what licenses they hold. Are they registered with the Better Business Bureau, or do they even have a business license? How far ahead are they booked? If you can see them right away, chances are they're not so good. After all, would you go to a doctor just because he or she has a flashing scalpel on a sign?

I'm reminded of the time several years ago when I was approached by a big producer to do a psychic hot line. The money would have been $40,000 a week to start, with an additional upward scale on every call that came in—which could have meant thousands of extra dollars per week depending on call volume.

I naïvely asked, "How can I answer all those phones and give the people enough time?"

He smiled like I was a dope. "You won't be doing that— you'll just write a script and lend your name to hundreds of people answering the phone."

I thought he was kidding, but quickly realized that he was dead serious. Now I'm not telling this because I need kudos, but in a split second, I saw all the people who believed in me and how hard it was to try to make this spiritual psychic journey authentic and for God. And then I saw the faces of my ministers and Grandma Ada. It was a time when I was barely making staff payroll, but what would it have ended up costing me to sink to that level? I couldn't say no fast enough (as my oldest son will attest to because he was with me), and felt lucky to have narrowly avoided this psychic attack.

Speaking of which, psychic attacks are more bad energy than actual attacks. For example, there are people out there who can drain you or make you feel uneasy. Take your first impression and run, or at least avoid them. They may not want to overtly hurt you, but in all probability, they wouldn't be good for you. I've been subjected to such attacks, and they can hit before you realize it. It's that what's-the-use feeling, the worthlessness and even depression that can come over you. As soon as you feel this, it can be like a tape that plays and plays—so eject it. Just place it, along with your so-called demons, in a box and blow it up . . . your soul will soar.

* * * * * *

TENET XII

The body is a living temple unto God, wherein we worship the spark of the Divine.

Jesus, Buddha, Mohammed, and other religious leaders have all stated that the body is a temple. At Novus Spiritus, we believe that the body houses the soul, and what seems to be so temporary and fragile is probably one of the biggest miracles that God has created. People who don't believe in God need only look at this wonderful creation that comes from *a single* egg and sperm and becomes this perfect machine (as it were).

Even if science discovers how to clone the human body, they'll only be copying what's already been created by God. Personally, I'm not thrilled about the cloning aspect, but I know that if God doesn't want it, it will fail. It almost seems as if humankind wants to *be* God, not be part of Him/Her. And as for stem-cell research, I favor it, but why not use the umbilical cords? There are certainly enough of them without harvesting embryos.

Anyway, we should honor and care for this temple we live in because life is a miracle. Yet when we become addicted to harmful substances (which seems to be an astronomically growing problem), we defile our temple. Now there are probably as many reasons for addiction as there are substances to be addicted to. It can strike anywhere, and we all probably know someone who has such a problem. In fact, we all have some kind of addiction ourselves—for example, mine is coffee, which I've had to cut down on (too much acid—damn!); other people find themselves continually craving chocolate or soda. These are the "lesser addictions," which I'll address in a bit. Right now I'd like to tackle the really lethal addictions: those related to alcohol and drugs.

Drugs and alcohol have been with us in some form as far back as recorded history—and beyond. For example, hashish and peyote have been used by witch doctors and shamans for centuries to put them in an altered state (yet they tended to only be used at certain times for tribal rituals). Many workers in South America are given coca leaves or beans, which is where cocaine comes from, so they'll work harder and longer with no sleep. And in America, we've dealt with all kinds of drugs, including LSD. Originally concocted by doctors to explore the recesses of the mind, LSD somehow got into the mainstream and was used widely in the hippie days. It started out as peace and love, but like all things taken to excess, by the 1970s it had begun to spread like a cancer (along with cocaine abuse). Dr. Timothy Leary didn't help matters any by extolling the virtues of mind-altering drugs.

It was almost as if we were trying to escape the horrors of our society (at that time we were dealing with Vietnam). I'm sure that there have always been pockets of substance abusers all across the country, but mainstream-media attention was soon focused on drugs . . . and has yet to let up.

Substance abuse used to be hushed up among the upper crust and the rich and famous, but even that eventually became news—especially now that we hear so much about celebrities and their addictions. Rush Limbaugh; Nick Nolte; Bobby Brown; Whitney Houston; Courtney Love; Robert Downey, Jr.; and others have generated headlines in recent years, and that was just the tip of the iceberg. Even Ray Charles, who was a wonderful talent, was bedeviled by heroin—but fortunately was able to kick the habit long before he died. Sadly, the same cannot be said for John Belushi, River Phoenix, Judy Garland, Marilyn Monroe, Jerry Garcia, Kurt Cobain, Jimi Hendrix, Janis Joplin, Chris Farley, or Elvis Presley . . . and the list goes on.

We're in the process of making our way through this world, and if we don't face life full on, we'll just have to come back and repeat the whole process. Whether people realize it or not, addiction to alcohol and drugs is a type of subliminal suicide. I know that life isn't easy, but it can't be any harder than having the proverbial monkey on your back as you wait for that next drink or fix.

Peer pressure is very strong, especially among our youth. Some of us remember when beer was the only choice—now we have drugs on the street that we can't even pronounce. But it's not just kids who are in danger. I talk to men and women every day who are hooked on painkillers, uppers, downers, and on and on it goes. And I know about this silent, creeping cancer firsthand because my mother was a prescription-drug addict (and I'm not blaming her doctors for this, since she went "doctor shopping"). Yet I do thank God for the one good thing I got out of this: I hate drugs and can't drink!

Think of it this way—why would anyone want to live in a filthy house with mold and scum? Yet that's essentially how many of us treat our temples. As my grandmother used to say, you can be poor, but you don't have to be dirty. And our outward living conditions do tend to be an example of what's going on inside. As I mentioned earlier, Grandma Ada lived in one room of a condemned building, yet it was spotless. She bought paint and fixed up the rusted iron bed; she also made doilies for the dresser, and dyed sheets to make curtains. Her space was sparsely furnished, but it was clean and cozy. My son Chris takes after her in this way. His house is immaculate, and I think I drive him crazy because I'm a collector and have knickknacks all over my home. And my son Paul is also clean, but he's more laid-back about it.

Then I have a dear friend who's spotless about her person, but her house is a pigsty. I find it phenomenal that she can reside in a place that has no semblance of order. Of course, I have to admit that I can be the opposite. As my dad used to tease me, "Why don't you have a mop tied to your butt so that you can do two things at once?" I've gotten better, especially when I realized that people didn't necessarily feel comfortable in my home. If they smoked, for example, I was immediately cleaning their ashtrays—it's a wonder I wasn't dusting my guests off, too.

After I divorced my first husband, my neat-freak tendencies calmed down. I now see that I was trying to bring order to my marriage, which was completely in chaos. I tried to at least have some control over my outward environment, if not my internal sadness. So it can be easy to keep the outward temple in order, but the real test is the inner temple.

Now don't get me wrong—there's nothing wrong with taking prescription drugs as long as they're not abused. I mean, who would deny that a diabetic needs insulin or that all manner of illnesses have been treated with medications that have saved countless lives? I'm talking about the *abuse* of substances here. For example, I saw a housewife on Dr. Phil's show who took 30 to 40 painkillers *a day,* and she was forced to sell her possessions to feed her habit. (Meanwhile, I threw up and came down with a horrible rash after taking one single Vicodin!) Someone who's taking this many pills is hiding from herself and trying to cope with a world or situation, past or present, that she feels she can't deal with . . . and she's not alone.

Countless people abuse themselves with drugs or alcohol, regardless of what it does to their brains or organs, or what laws they have to break in the process. The substance becomes the master; and the addict has to steal, prostitute themselves, or do any manner of illegal activity to get what their system cries out for. But it doesn't last . . . the fix wears off, and the vicious cycle begins all over again. Addicts like to say, "Just one more time and then I'm done." Then the guilt sets in; and they feel hopeless, helpless, and debased because of their weakness.

Addiction can also bring about changes in behavior. How many times have you heard a person say, "He's a completely different person when he drinks"? Addicts commit acts that they'd never do if they were sober, such as abusing their spouses or children. Some don't care, but the majority really do hate their lifestyle yet feel trapped by their addictions. Often addicts will say that they're embarrassed by their weakness—well, there's nothing weak about sitting through an intervention from family and friends, checking into a rehab facility, or going to see a doctor who can provide the right treatment. Substance abusers not only need help from friends and family, they need medical attention, too.

If you're involved with an addict who doesn't accept your help, keep in mind that there are so many out there who *do* need and want your assistance, so don't waste your time and energy on those who can't or won't be helped . . . no matter how much you love them. I'm reminded of a woman I talked to once who was half-crazy because she'd put her son in rehab ten times, only to have him come out and get back on heroin—the same day—every time. This was an incredibly sad situation, but I had to gently tell her that there comes a time when we realize that we have to give up because the drug has beaten not only our loved one, but us, too.

And then there's St. Monica, who prayed for 17 years that her son, the future St. Augustine, would give up his ways of debauchery. I don't mean to seem hateful, but it seemed that he finally did so when he was too old to party anymore—and then he wrote about how putrid mankind was. I admire the fact that he gave up his lifestyle, but I wish that he would have come out of his darkness to give hope instead of telling us that our temple was rotten. Certainly we get old and things break down—sure, a rose doesn't last forever, but at least while it does, it brings beauty, joy, and fragrance. Better to be of an ephemeral use than crabgrass that kills off the lawn, I say.

＊ ＊ ＊

Now I'd like to shift the focus to those addictions that don't center around drugs or alcohol. For example, many people have obsessions with sex and pornography, which cause widespread infidelity. Such behavior not only disrespects the person you've chosen to be with, it also debases the very essence of *your* being.

Our Lord is very specific on this in Matthew 19:3–5: "And there came to him the Pharisees tempting him, and saying: 'Is it lawful for a man to put away his wife for every cause?' Who answering, said to them: 'Have ye not read, that He who made man from the beginning, made them male and female?' And he said: 'For this cause shall a man leave father and mother, and shall cleave to his wife, and they two shall be in one flesh.'"

Jesus later states that the only reason for divorce is sexual infidelity. Even back then he was trying to keep families together and wasn't accepting divorce. (Moses, on the other hand, did believe in putting away a bad spouse by divorce.) I divorced my first husband because after 13 years I couldn't stand the physical and mental abuse. I felt my own temple was crumbling, so I went to see a priest at the Queen of Apostles Church, where I was working as a schoolteacher. I was wringing my hands out of panic, yet I told him about the abuse and my desire to divorce—which, of course, was not allowed by the Catholic Church except under extreme circumstances.

The priest looked at me long and hard and gravely said, "Sylvia, you have to leave for yourself, as well as your boys—

or they're going to believe that it is right for a man to treat a woman like this."

I just stared back at him, for that was the last thing I thought I'd hear. I did leave with my kids in tow, and even though Gary threatened to kill us, I held firm and got my divorce. I will be forever grateful to that priest for giving me the courage to leave and go on with my life. I had to get away for survival, but the key phrase was not just for me, but *for my children.* After all, a lioness will protect her cubs at all costs.

Food can also be an addiction for some people, and we've all heard the statistics about the frightening increase in obesity levels in this country. I feel that people are just eating more these days to fill the empty hole inside that only spirituality can address, and also I feel that this hole is homesickness for the Other Side. It doesn't take a rocket scientist to see that as the world gets more hectic, people find relief in what they call "comfort food."

Personally, I prefer a high-protein diet. In fact, long before Atkins ever wrote his book, Francine told me that if I didn't start to feed my body what it's made of, I'd get all types of immune diseases. Now that doesn't mean that we can't eat soy or protein substitutes, but remember—we have canine teeth, not flat teeth like herbivores. People tell me that they can't eat any living creature because it's "cruel," but let me tell you, plants literally scream when you cut them! Then we have the fanatics who only eat sprouts, exercise six hours a day, meditate for another three, and take everything to the extreme. It's much better if you just *do everything in moderation.* Eat right, sleep well, exercise, and fill your mind with good thoughts, and illness won't get in.

I've never been a fanatic about my body, but I do try to look and feel as good as my age—or any age—allows me to. Yes, I've had a facial peel and veneers put on my teeth. I get massages and facials when I can, and I try to walk daily (as if I'm not running through every airport!). I get my hair and nails done regularly, which might be considered vanity, but

I just feel better if I outwardly can show what I feel inside. I have low blood pressure and low blood sugar, so I have to eat often. I stay pretty much on protein—not a lot of red meat, but fish, turkey, eggs, and chicken—and vegetables. Starches could be my downfall, but I try to stay away from them. I have an occasional glass of wine, but I really don't drink because I get sick and don't like the smell of booze. That's probably a blessing, as so many psychics have been addicted to alcohol. I'm not judging here, as I'm sure it comes from the tension of their lives.

It does make me crazy when people tell me that I look tired or sick or that my voice sounds like I have an upper-respiratory disease. I guess that means all the women in my family did, for they had similar voices and lived to be in their 80s and 90s. It's funny, though—my dad used to call when he was out of town, and if I answered instead of my sister or mother, he'd ask, "Who is this?"

I'd reply in my girlish and docile way, "Who in the hell do you think it is?" And he'd laugh and say, "Oh, it's you, Sylvia."

Those who know me or have seen me on TV for years never ask if I'm feeling well, it's just well-meaning strangers who do so. But remember, it's just as easy to say, not only to me but to everyone, that someone looks good instead of planting a negative thought—no matter how well-meaning you might think it is.

How Can This Tenet Help You?

Buddha said, "Worldly desires are always seeking chances to deceive the mind. If a viper lives in your room and you wish to have a peaceful sleep, you must first chase it out. You must break the bonds of worldly passions and drive them away, as you would a viper. You must protect your mind." Or, as Nancy Reagan said, "Just say no."

There has to be some control learned here. We're all

subjected to the temptations of this feel-good society, yet the abuse can crumble our temple. We tell ourselves, "I'm stronger than this; I can try it and then give it up when I choose." Wrong! As any drug addict or alcoholic will tell you, it's like a viper that not only lives in your room, but in your mind and soul as well. No matter if it's a drink, a puff, a pill, or a snort, you'll always want another one if you're prone to addiction. Don't be fooled by the few who can take a substance once and not be affected. Why take the chance?

You may be using any number of the excuses (which number in the thousands) that addicts trot out to explain the abuse of their bodies with drugs and alcohol: "I started drinking to impress my friends, and then I couldn't stop," "It runs in my family," "I was abused at an early age," "I wanted to be cool," "I was socially afraid, but drugs/drinking made me more outgoing," "The stress of my life drove me to it," "I couldn't sleep at night," "I couldn't get up and do my job," "I couldn't get along with my partner," and so on—the list is endless. Well, these are just crutches you're using to try to salvage the knowledge of the soul that knows that if you abuse your temple, you block grace.

Go back again and find when you took your first drink, puff, pill, or snort and recall what you were doing or feeling. I'm not talking about your saying "I just wanted to experiment" here. Go deeper . . . what was going on in your internal or external life that made you feel you needed it? What made you keep chasing that elusive high? Remember, the temple you've been defiling all these years doesn't just belong to you, but to God. If you had a beautiful home and rented it to tenants who destroyed it, how would you feel? Also, they'd be legally bound to make it right. So it is with your body: Spiritually, you must make it right.

The addictions of life, including the gratification of gambling, drinking, drugs, sexual infidelity, and anything else that debases or affects our temples or those of our loved ones stops spiritual growth. I don't mean that you have to live like a monk, but any type of excess will cause damage in one way or another. You don't need a pill to expand your mind—the highs of life are found in love and joy, marriage, the birth of a child, a new puppy, the hand of a friend, or a kind word in the dark.

Go back and unplug the reasons for feelings of unworthiness, despair, guilt, remorse, or just foolhardiness, and ask God (with the help of your friends and family and trained professionals) to regain your temple. Start *today,* not just at the beginning of a new year or some far-off, never-to-happen time. Do it now before you lay waste to this beautiful edifice that God made for you. After all, who are you to deform not only yourself, but your God within? And remember to keep your temple pure and in good condition by doing everything in moderation.

* * * * * *

TENET XIII

God does not create the adversities in life. By your own choice they exist to aid in your perfection.

Hindus don't dread death, nor do they believe in an external hell (unlike many Christians, unfortunately). However, they *do* believe in hellish states of mind brought on by fear, hate, jealousy, bigotry, anger, and the like . . . which brings us to this tenet.

Sikhism, which is an offshoot of Hinduism, advocates holistic life experiences—in work, worship, and service—in order to attain a perpetual union with God, while also creating a just social order in this world. Sikhs are enjoined to lead a wholesome lifestyle; and they have a long, celebrated heritage of speaking out against injustice and for the defenseless. Sikh doctrine dictates that all people have the right to follow their own path to God without condemnation or coercion from others. They're profoundly democratic and believe in civil rights and freedom of religion.

Gnosticism, which is one of the world's oldest philosophies, feels the same way and is very tolerant of the beliefs of others. It believes that everyone has to find their own way to an all-loving, perfect God. In fact, when you analyze the world's main religions, you see so many similarities. Most of them, for instance, teach no prejudice and concentrate on right actions. The Dharma Wheel, which represents the major belief of Buddha's Eightfold Path (encompassing right views, right intent, right speech, right conduct, right livelihood, right effort, right mindfulness, and right concentration), is a prime example.

Gnosticism goes a little further and addresses all these "right actions" by their motive or intent. After all, it does no good to do something without love and understanding. Gnosticism also explores the reason that we're all living such harsh lives—namely, we're honing our souls and learning to ascend to God with knowledge. If we feel that we're just pawns or victims of our lives, then we haven't gained knowledge the way we should. Sure, we learn, but doing so without understanding falls somewhat flat. It's so much more glorious to really *know* that we're perfecting our souls.

As I've mentioned before, Earth is the only "hell" there is. My spirit guide Francine says that there are millions of planets that are inhabited, but this is the only one that has evil and negativity in such abundance—and only the bravest of the brave incarnate here to face this planet's adversities. Earth is the toughest school in the universe, which is why so many of us come here.

We may often wonder why, if God is all-loving, He/She allows this planet and all of its suffering to exist. When Jesus went to the garden of Gethsemane and asked God to remove the pain of the crucifixion that he knew was coming, God essentially told him, "No—you chose it to be this way in your contract, so you have to see it through." We're fairly confident that this took place because we hear our Lord say with resignation and almost despair, "Thy will be done." Meaning that he knew he chose it, but he wasn't happy about it. It was his contract with God, which contained his messianic legacy to fulfill his chart. And if *he* couldn't get out of his contract, what hope do we have?

You see, what happens is when we're on the Other Side, we say, "Oh, I can handle that." We end up picking all sorts of hardships that, in this state of bliss, we feel we can handle to spiritually advance for God. Then we get down here and want to change the chart. Yes, we can modify it in minor ways, but its major attributes can never be altered.

We end up picking a contract for a loving God without human qualities Who gives us a chance to learn what He/She already knows. It's very much like the symbology in Genesis when God declares that we learn by coming down and tilling the field and bearing our children in hardship after Adam and Eve eat from the apple of the Tree of Knowledge. Unfortunately, negativity is part of that knowledge, whether we like it or not. If we don't have any adversity, then we don't know what we're made of and can't advance our knowledge and soul.

This temporal plane of existence exists because God allows it to. As our Creator, God is also our Father and Mother. We who are parents can attest to letting our children venture out from home to learn, and it follows that our Creator would do the same thing, since He/She wants us to acquire knowledge.

Our kids are part of us, just as we're a part of God. Loving them, suffering for them when they make mistakes, and having empathy for their pain all comes with the territory of being a parent. And Shakespeare hit the nail on the head when he said, "How sharper than a serpent's tooth it is / To have a thankless child!" Speaking of this (and it's not just because I'm a mother), why is it that when a child goes off track, the first person the therapist looks at is the mother? True, she's the heart of the home, but what about a cruel, neglectful father?

Anyway, we parents try to make a home for our children that's secure, loving, and safe; and we try to protect them as much as possible, but we can't live their lives for them. Why would our Creator be any different? That's why the earthly plane is only a temporary stopover in our existence. The real reality is our Home on the Other Side, where it's a safe environment filled with nothing but love. There's no negativity or evil on the Other Side, and our Creator loves us so much that He/She makes *that* the real plane of existence for our souls.

Of course we've been told from ancient times that if the gods aren't appeased by sacrifice or penance (following human-made rules, I'd just like to add), we'll have all manner of strife befall us, from crops failing, pestilence, and war to having our loved ones being taken from us. In fact, in the not-so-distant past, you couldn't compliment a baby for fear that either God or a so-called demon would be jealous and take it. And my grandmother used to tell me that when she was a child, she was told that if you love something too much it will be taken from you. Naturally, she knew this was nonsense, but it illustrates how ignorance can poison us all. I cannot stress enough that God does not create the negativity in our lives—*we do.*

We've all experienced joyous births, heart-wrenching deaths, lost friendships, being defamed or deceived by others, hardship, pain, illness, surgery, getting old, and myriad other facets of life . . . yet all are part of the learning process. Often it can feel like giving birth: My son Christopher, for instance, was an eight-pound, premature baby who took 36 hours to deliver. Believe me, I wasn't having a good time. Nevertheless, as soon as I saw him, I forgot all about the pain and found joy in what I'd gone through to get this prize. So life goes.

I have two wonderful sons and three amazing grandkids . . . and terrible taste in men. I've lost so many I love to the Other Side, and it seems that the number grows each day. My sons and I even went through divorces almost simultaneously—Chris's was first, and then Paul's and mine happened at about the same time. This was all as recent as three years ago, and there were days when I was seeing all parties suffer so much that I thought I couldn't bear it. It was one of those times when you want to scream, "What next?!" But now the grandchildren are fine and very well adjusted. My boys have wonderful partners now, and I still love and see both of my former daughters-in-law.

So many times we wonder why, if we're following our path correctly, it can't be easier. The bumps in my road have certainly aggravated me—after all, I'm human. At such "lost moments" I've even told God, "Okay, that's enough . . . I got it! Maybe I charted for rain, but I didn't expect a flood!" But then Francine will say, "Well, if you're going to learn it, Sylvia, learn it right." She can really be aggravating at times. Yes, she's right, and I love her, but I'm like anyone else and don't always like the truth.

When tragedies happen, it's natural to ask, "Why me?" Well, why not you? Each one of us wrote our charts in order to perfect. It's just that when we get into it, we decide that we don't want to do it. I find it really interesting, though, that humankind doesn't seem to want to take responsibility for any part of our lives and would rather blame things on God. We give our souls to dogma, entrust our bodies to doctors, and put our finances in others' hands. Some people even have their own personal shoppers! We can't seem to do anything for ourselves anymore—no wonder we often feel helpless and useless.

I purposely tend my own garden and do my own sewing—along with all the other things I've always done. I had my grandkids at Wal-Mart recently, and at least ten people approached me and said, "I can't believe you're here!" Why? I have to be somewhere. (I've also gotten that same response at Denny's.) I don't have to be at Spago or Louis Vuitton. I'm not against anyone who does frequent those places, but I happen to love the bargains at Wal-Mart, and my grandchildren enjoy it there, too. And I buy a lot of my clothes at a little shop in Santa Monica called Gioia where Laura, the owner, saves what she thinks I'll like, and I usually do.

I'm including these little vignettes to show you how "average" minutes, hours, and days stack up to make a life. Remember, your motive for how you handle your life is always and forever between you and God. Every minute of our lives is meant to improve us—we just have to remember to look at it that way.

The one facet of my personality I've really had to work on is my temper. I was always in the principal's office, especially in grade school. I'm sure that today they'd say I had ADD or ADHD, since I wasn't much for sitting still. Although I always got good grades, I preferred to pass the time in class passing notes, talking, and telling stories to everyone. God bless the nuns—they'd roll their eyes and do the best they could with me.

Getting back to my temper, I remember when I was in the sixth grade and my sister was in kindergarten—she came crying to me about a girl named Sheila who'd taken her lunch money. Well, I caught Sheila after school and smashed inchworms (which hung off trees in Missouri) in her hair. Back to the principal's office I went. And when I was in the seventh grade, I was on the girls' softball team. A player from another team called me a "Jew bitch," and before I knew it I had her on the ground and the battle was on.

I did learn over the years, with my grandmother's admonitions, that nothing is accomplished by physical retaliation, even though I certainly felt that justice had been served with inchworms and fists. Usually my ire comes to the foreground when someone I love is hurt. Touch what I love and my mouth lets loose.

Speaking of my mouth, I've been criticized for being a little too "colorful" in my language. Some would like me to be saintlier in my speech when I lecture or answer questions, while others love the way that I tell it like it is. No matter if you love me or hate me, I am who I am, and I just don't believe that God is going to fault me for speaking the way I do—after all, it doesn't take away from my spirituality.

Some people have mistaken my honesty for sarcasm.

Now this doesn't mean that I'm never sarcastic, but I don't use such a tone in my psychic work. I give no excuses, but I've run several businesses as a woman alone, so I've had to live by my wits. It's enough to be stereotyped in business, but I'm blonde and have an endowed chest, so does that make me dumb?

Nevertheless, all of the put-downs I've received over the years—along with all of the good words and love—have helped me fulfill my chart. No matter how small or large an incident may be, it serves to bring us the lessons we need. The road is filled with heartaches and adversities that we've chosen, but there are also so many moments of love and happiness.

In school we can't just go and bitch to the counselor, especially when we picked the classes to graduate. Life is the same way: Why blame God for what *we* chose to complete? If we take a more optimistic view of our perception of life, we'll find that the world becomes less adversarial. Yet some individuals can't enjoy the good times and keep waiting for the other shoe to drop.

It's amazing how many people can't savor the precious moments of life, especially those spent with loved ones. These are so much more valuable than any material thing. I'm immediately reminded of the time I was sitting with my granddaughter about four years ago after we'd spent the day shopping (we even got a rabbit!). We were sitting at the kitchen table eating our favorite salad, when Angelia looked at me and said, "This was a perfect day."

I said, "Yes, it was, darling. Save it in your mind because when life gets hard, you can take it out and it will make your heart glow." *Good God,* I realized, *I've become Grandma Ada!* Yet these are the memories and treasures that we take with us.

The hardest thing for you and me to swallow is that we're the ones responsible for our charts, especially if they seem really rotten. We may wonder, *Why did I write one thing and want another?* Well, some of us recall a past time when we were happier, or we remember the Other Side where things are perfect. This leaks through and makes us homesick.

I really thought that I just wanted to have children, stay home, and have a man take care of me. Things didn't turn out exactly as I planned, but then would I have been really happy? Probably not. Would I have liked to have given my children more time? Yes, but the time I gave them was quality. Did my dream of being taken care of come true? No, I always supported everyone, even my husbands. Yet do I regret that? No. As I look back, I remember what my ex-boyfriend Joe once told me: "The world called." The need to support has also given me the impetus and will to continue.

With much gut-wrenching work, I've made baby steps to find what Sylvia wants. Yes, I have to live by my chart, but I also try to be good to *me* in the process. I won't say that I've always been thrilled with my fate, but I did have choices (not so much externally, but internally), and so do you.

How Can This Tenet Help You?

Life is circles within circles: You come in and go back and make the rounds again until you go Home and stay there. I know that you've probably felt abandoned like Job in the Bible—you feel that God has ignored you, let things happen to you, or created them to happen. None of that is true. So instead of blaming God for the adversity you picked, blame *yourself* for not handling it with grace and dignity. Even if you have to grit your teeth and bear it at times, at least when you get to the Other Side you can know that you did give it your all.

The "poor me" syndrome just brings more negativity to

your doorstep. It builds upon itself until you're buried in a sea of self-pity or the feeling of "Why has God done this to me?" Until you break this pattern, you'll always feel self-defeated, and the strength God gave you will diminish in your soul. You'll feel abandoned and alone and will be apt to say something like, "What did I ever do in this life, or any other life, to be punished like this?" You haven't done anything—except perhaps take on a difficult chart to learn and graduate and advance your soul, which is in a very temporary body.

Now, just as I'm working to improve my temper, you also have facets of your personality that you must overcome. In other words, it isn't just the adversities of life you must face, but also those inside *yourself.* It's truly not only what you go through, but how you handle it, too. The outward world is just a proving ground, but you're the one who's here to test your inner essence or soul to see how you overcome such obstacles.

It's true that now I find more people on their last lives than I have in the last 20 years—and I'm one of them. There could be two reasons for this. One is that people are merely finished—that is, they're tired of this world that has beauty, but which also has so much hate, war, stress, cruelty, and so forth. So many people whom I talk to on the phone, when I tell them it's their last life, say in one form or another, "Oh, thank God! I just knew it, and I don't want to come here again." I myself have frequently said that we're coming to the end of days.

The other reason is that I think many people have had a lot of lives and feel ready to graduate. It's like school: You may find it hard at times. You may enjoy some classes, but others you hate or fail and have to take over again; or you feel that your grade wasn't an accurate indicator of what you can do, so you try harder. I hated math, especially algebra, but with tutoring I got through it. I never used it and didn't really master it, but by sheer determination I passed the damn course. School was a test of agony, tenacity, and patience, but there were wonderful classes, too: English, drama, humanities, and history were all stimulating for me. When you're ready to graduate, just like in life, you're anxious to start another facet of your true existence (like going Home). Your lessons have been learned, and reality begins.

It's said that we should seize the day. Well, I say seize the *moment*. There really is so much beauty, glory, and love around you, but you're passing it up by focusing on self-pity. It's all so simple: God is truly in His/Her heaven (and ours), and everything will ultimately be all right in your world. If it isn't so externally, then make sure that it is internally. When you take your adversity and stare it down, you'll come out the winner—especially if you keep telling yourself, as all the prophets and messengers have, that this is a transient place, and you'll soon be going Home.

So stand tall, muster up some courage and dignity, and face this difficult world with your chin high. Know that you *are* going to get through it!

* * * * * *

TENET XIV

Karma is nothing more than honing the wheel of evolvement. It is not retribution, but merely a balancing of experiences.

*K*arma is a word that has been so bandied about that its true meaning has become muddled. It actually just means to experience for your soul in this life and many others . . . no more, no less. Yet the word was subsequently interpreted by Eastern religions to mean that whatever you put out (especially if it's negative) will come back to you manyfold—and they didn't go further to explain that bad actions only come back *when they're done with malice*. Finally, as the New Age (I hate that expression) arrived, "karma" seemed to be adopted by neophytes who thought that they truly knew what the word meant and carried it to the extreme. *Everything* seemed to be laced with karmic over- or undertones.

I remember one time, for instance, when I was invited by a spiritual group to present some pointers on healing and meditation. After sitting on the floor for a long time, I said, "Oh, I'm so stiff I can barely get up!"

The man next to me was named Charles, and he quickly responded, "Don't put that out in the ethers [atmosphere] or it will karmically come true!"

"Get real, Charles," I shot back. "That's silly. I'm not going to monitor every word I say for some definition of *karma* that's totally erroneous." It's no wonder that some of these New Age groups are considered strange!

People get so bound up in dogma or some type of false spiritual decorum that they forget that God knows their hearts and intentions. In fact, sin and karma seem to be sisters. The origin of the word *sin* means to just miss the mark; while if you miss the experience of learning, karma will make sure that it comes again. Consider this: It's the realization that we've missed the learning experience that makes us go back to try to fix something or make up for it. If we can't mend that particular situation, then we tend to pick the one closest to it and address that. For example, I couldn't fix my mother no matter what I did, but I used her example to fix *me* so that I wouldn't ever be like her.

I'm sure you've noticed that if you try to dodge the bullet of learning, it will come again. As I've said before, life is circles within circles, and many times we end up where we started—but hopefully we're wiser and have gained more grace and spirituality. In many East Indian religions, the wheel of karma never seems to stop: Some Hindus and Buddhists, for instance, believe that the wheel of life keeps turning to the point that some people live thousands of lives.

All I can say (not to be critical or disparaging) is that logically you'd have to always come back into life immediately after death, and no one would be able to get you on the Other Side. You'd always be on a journey of coming and going, so you'd never be able to reside at the Home from whence you came. You wouldn't even have the time to regroup and see what you wanted to accomplish next time.

Now in all my 50 years of research, in which my ministers and I have personally done thousands of past-life regressions (including many on individuals from Eastern religions), never once have we found anyone who has lived thousands and thousands of lives.

During these regressions, I've also failed to find anyone who has experienced the transmigration of their soul. Many Eastern religions believe in this concept, which is basically living a life (or lives) in the body of another living creature, such as a cow, insect, dog, cat, rat, or what have you. This belief has direct tie-ins not only to karma, but also to the caste system that was in place just decades ago (and is still practiced unofficially in many places).

To try to simplify it as much as possible, this goes back to the belief that karma dictates how you're going to live your next life: If you lead a good one, you'll go upward in the caste system in your next life; but if you don't, you're going to go downward to possibly become an "untouchable" (lowest caste of human life) or even an animal or insect in your next life. This is one of the reasons why animals and insects are never killed intentionally in countries such as India. Citizens believe that they might be killing a soul who's trying to get to the point of perfection in which they can live a human life—thus, they'd incur their own karma for interfering. These people seem to take karma to its extreme definition, just as they do reincarnation.

Well, I'm here to tell you that an animal has no agenda except to live by pure instinct, love, and even honor. Yes, it's a shame that we don't come back as cats or dogs and learn what pure, uncomplicated survival means, but God created animals without any karma. In fact, they're a separate species unto themselves for humankind, both as a help (food, balance of nature, pollination, and so forth) and a hindrance (disease, crop destruction, and the like) to help us perfect our souls. Just as angels are separate creations from spirit guides or ghosts, the animal kingdom was created to help in the evolution of the planet and humankind—not as vehicles for us to live lives in.

We only incarnate in human form, but many times society has its way of forming barriers due to religious practices.

Taking the aforementioned caste system as an example, religious belief dictated that those in the lower classes wouldn't be as evolved as those in the upper classes. The untouchables were considered to be very unevolved souls in comparison to the upper castes, so they were relegated to the harshest menial labor and its subsequent outcome: poverty. Hinduism is considered to be one of the world's oldest active religions, and its teachings have influenced every major religion today—but it has also influenced today's society. The caste system (which was outlawed a few decades ago due to pressure from human-rights activists) is really no different from the delineation of classes of people today, as we have the poor, the middle class, and the rich . . . and that's it.

It's so wrong for people to always use karma as an excuse for everything—especially when past lives and cell memory more often come into play. Many times in a past life we'll have had a negative experience with drowning, snakes, heights, choking, closed-in places, and so forth; consequently, they become left over in our cell memory. Then, when we come into this life, that cell memory is often still active and affects us, but it has nothing to do with being punished for a bad action.

For example, in one of my past lives I was an empress who was poisoned. This memory had invaded my cells to the point that when I was very tiny, I wouldn't eat anything my mother gave me until my dad or someone else tasted it first. I haven't investigated it, but perhaps my mother or someone close poisoned me in that life and it was a carry-over. I eventually got over this fear with my grandma's help, when she very matter-of-factly explained that that was then and this is now.

Also, six lives before this one, I didn't have any children because I was an oracle who couldn't marry. In other lives, I was a spinster in Poland who was the last daughter and had to take care of aging parents, a young girl in Kenya who died early, and a nun. So in this life, I wanted children more than anything—it was my need and karmic experience to do so.

On the other hand, I have two friends who had so many children in past lives that this is the last thing they wanted in this life.

Now the reason we pick so many lives (and we white entities usually do) is *not* because we've done something terrible or have incurred karma. Instead, we usually feel that we could have handled a situation much better, so we try it again to make sure that we've gotten out of it what we needed. We also might feel that we have to learn a certain hardship or experience sorrow or even violence to perfect our soul. Maybe we choose an early death to bring others to spirituality and awareness, or we want to be kinder and more patient—the list could go on endlessly. Unlike this life, when we say, "If I had it to do over again, I would have done such and such," reincarnation allows us many chances to do what we didn't do according to our own karmic experience for God.

So when life gets bad, we shouldn't immediately jump to the false conclusion that "I must have been terrible in a past life." It's more that we're just working out a balancing of our experience and knowledge. And as hard as it is to understand, people do karmically come down to create a greater good through suffering. The incident of 9/11 was an example of that. Those incredible people didn't die in vain; rather, they were like saints who chose to show us that this country was far too complacent. They were like a type of Paul Revere, warning that the enemy was coming in the form of terrorism. In Hitler's time, the blessed souls who died in concentration camps made the world turn their attention not only to the Nazis' atrocities, but also to what horror can be done in the name of bigotry and insane prejudice.

On the Other Side, when we're happy and in "bliss" (a term often used by Joseph Campbell), we feel so good that we pick all types of charts for the realization and betterment of the whole human race. Those who choose charts full of suffering are truly our saintly martyrs. The countless people who were either burned at the stake or tortured and killed in the Inquisition by the Catholic Church are examples of those who died in martyrdom and innocence. (It's no wonder why anyone with any type of healing ability or second sight kept it hidden!) Everyone, no matter who they are, has their own experience to fulfill their chart for God. It seems senseless to us here because we sometimes forget (myself included) to look at the bigger picture. We all come into life for a very short period of time in comparison to eternity, and we choose different lessons to bring about a better and greater good.

* * *

Kenyans are firm believers in the type of karma in which what is sent out comes back, even though most of them are practicing Christians. And here I'd like to digress for a moment.

It's true that there are places in the world that if we're fortunate to find them, they'll help bring peace to our soul. For me, that place is Kenya, which is a spiritual home for me. I've been there many times, but the world and my work has crowded in so much that I can't take the time to go back as much as I'd like. Nevertheless, that country is forever with me. When I stepped off the plane on my first visit in 1980, I said, "Oh God, I'm home."

The smells, the dear animals, and the smiling faces of everyone you see are unbelievable. They have the most incredible sky there . . . you can actually touch the clouds. The light at sunset is a golden orange, with the animals silhouetted against the growing night sky. Even if you're having tea at the old Norfolk Hotel, as I was with Christina Kenyatta (daughter of the first president of Kenya), and have a serious expression on your face, you're apt to have an attendant come up and say, "Mama, are you not happy? Can I make you happy?"

I often half-jokingly say that the problem is that God *lives* in Africa and only *visits* other places. So when I get a little down, I think of when I was sitting under a baobab tree writing with Samson, a German shepherd, sitting at my feet—I think that this is as close to the Other Side as I will get on this earth.

I also try to remind myself that to be in a state of stupor doesn't allow us to perfect anything. There's an old saying that's trite but true: "What comes too easy probably shouldn't be trusted." I found this to be reliable in my life, as I'm sure you have. That's not to say that opportunity will never drop in your lap, but generally it will be because prior to this, you paid your dues.

For example, let's look at the "overnight success." Usually this person has toiled for years before he or she gets noticed. For example, I was 36 before I got my first TV interview and didn't write my first book until I was 50—but I'd been doing readings and oftentimes was the local oddity since I was 18 years old. So you see what it takes to become an overnight success. Of course, some of the younger stars who quickly do become sensations often have their lives turn upside down later. They live as if their fame and fortune will go on forever, and it doesn't. So many become penniless, addicted to drugs or alcohol, have run-ins with the law, and so on.

Step by step, we all make it to the top of our karmic or experiencing ladder, and the hardships of that journey can often be what save us when we finally get there. Our karmic path will get us to our appointed destiny if we just take it with slow strides and never demean or step on anyone, or use them to get ahead. We can never put ourselves above others, because we're all on the same journey and have all had a chance to be someone of importance. Even if we live a simple life, we're all famous in God's eyes.

There can also be group karma, in which many people experience for a cause or truth together. More than once, members of my study groups—and all of my ministers—have jokingly told me, "I know you talked us into this Gnostic mission on the Other Side, and you were so persuasive that we went along with you." They've even threatened to run from me when we all get back Home, just in case I get it into my head to come back and make sure that what we started continues properly!

It's true I always fear that after I'm gone my words will get misinterpreted, as those from so many messengers from God have over time. But I know that Chris, my youngest, will carry on just like Hugh Lynn Cayce did after his dad, Edgar, passed on.

The group-karma experience is usually wider in scope than the individual experience, but it's not a lesser or greater one. We truly are our brother's keeper, which means that we're all tied together in a great "karmic jigsaw." In other words, what you think is unfair is actually fair, and what injustices you see have been chosen by the brave souls who've come to show us what the human spirit can survive and learn from. People on the Other Side are also learning by watching us go through our tribulations, so when we get back Home we'll share our experiences and will even help others write their charts accordingly.

Now, as I've already mentioned, sometimes we choose too much because we're so enthusiastic on the Other Side—then we come down here and the full impact of what we've chosen hits us like a two-by-four. I know that I've certainly felt like this a time or two. "If you live long enough," my grandmother used to say, "you'll see it all." That's so true.

We may think that we have a choice when these deaths, deceptions, divorces, and illnesses happen, but we don't. So we pick up the pieces of our lives and superglue them back together with every spiritual part of our being, and we get up and (for a while) painfully go on until time heals the wounds. While nothing may be able to give us solace at this time, one day we wake up and the lights go on again. We may never truly stop the pain of the loss, but we can eventually turn it into sympathy and understanding for others and a deeper understanding of ourselves and the strength we have.

We all share the experience of karma and learning . . .

hopefully, we can do it with dignity and spiritual strength. I know that I work toward it every day, knowing that total understanding and peace is not for here, but for our heavenly Home. And I also know that our Creator never says that He/She is disappointed in us, but it's the God within all of us that stretches for perfection in this life—and can sometimes be our harshest critic. Of course we fall at times, but we'll get up and make it better, in this life or the next. Most entities are on their last life or two, so that's why we're seeing such a search for truth today.

To release karma, we don't need to use sage, crystals, or cards; meditate for hours; or cleanse ourselves through various methods. We simply need to do the best we can and make it through the adversities and good times of life. And remember, we never stop learning—not even on the Other Side.

How Can This Tenet Help You?

I started this book in Hawaii, and now I'm on the *Mississippi Queen* riverboat giving lectures and readings and continuing my writing. I love to see the different cultures within our own country, but one thing I've found in all my travels here and abroad is that people are searching for spirituality, and it's as individual as our looks. I had someone on the river cruise, for instance, come up to me and say, "The Bible doesn't mention 'karma.'"

I politely replied, "I beg to differ, but there is no finer example of karma then when our Lord said, 'Do unto others as you would have them do unto you.'"

I hardly ever get aggravated with people because (and I'm not trying to sound like Bill Clinton here) I feel their pain, but once in a while, I'm human and my nerves just go. And there are some people I simply can't please or give enough to, so it's better to just let it go. Now you might feel karmically attached to your family, friends, and co-workers and try and try to please them. Well, if they can't accept all that you do or have done, then just go, or let them go because this isn't your karma, it's theirs.

Now to truly comprehend the concept of karma, you have to understand its universal rule: to live life to the fullest and care about others *as well as yourself*. Don't let the past cripple you, don't let guilt overcome you, and quit obsessing about what you did or didn't do—it's dead, wasted energy. Then you start carrying around your own heavy armor of karma that you've forged in the fire of your personal fears and misgivings. This will make you sick, depressed, and tired . . . and your life will hold no joy at all.

Karma simply means that you're completing the themes you chose for learning, so stop with "What did I do so terribly wrong that I'm being punished this time?" In the first place, only good people say this—dark souls never give it a thought because they think they're perfect. Also, dark-soul entities have to keep coming back to this hellhole and never get to the Other Side like we do. To me, that's the best karma of all.

Francine says that it usually takes five years for karma to enact, especially when something has been done to you out of maliciousness and premeditated intent. Now some of you will say, "I've waited 10 or 20 years for a crime to be solved, or for someone who has hurt me or my family to receive their just due, so what gives?" Well, many times you won't hear about what's happened to these people; or, from the outside things may look great for them, but inside I can tell you that they're definitely not.

Don't be concerned if you think negative thoughts about the individual who hurt you, because it's a human reaction that has no effect on him or her. Remember, curses don't work. Don't get me wrong—anyone can absorb negative and positive energy emanating from someone in close proximity, and thoughts are things that have energy, but the average human being doesn't have the time, power, or concentration to project thoughts that harm another.

However, God has given all of us an innate defensive system that wards off most negativity—unless you leave yourself open to receive it. This accounts for the rare and isolated cases in certain cultures in which a person believes that they're cursed (making them open to negativity), and then they get sick or die as a result of that belief.

Yes, the mind is very powerful, and you can heal or hurt yourself depending on the power of your belief. In either case, *you're* the one doing it, not anyone else. Keep in mind that what is purposely sent out comes back. If you've lost your husband to another woman, you might want them both dead, but that is an emotional human reaction—with time, it will cool. Now if you hire a hit man to take care of the wayward spouse, that would incur karma coming back to *you*.

I know that karma can sometimes be a fine line to understand, but we *are* allowed to hate evil and evil actions. When this world ends, God in His/Her mercy and love will absorb all of the dark entities back into His/Her mass, while we will stay as ourselves and reap the rewards from the Other Side. That certainly sounds like good karma to me.

✳ ✳ ✳ ✳ ✳ ✳

TENET XV

*God allows each person the
opportunity for perfection, whether
you need one life or a hundred lives
to reach your level of perfection.*

Just as we choose different themes or lessons that we're going to learn, we also pick the number of lives (and even the years, months, days, and hours) that we're going to exist on this planet in order to complete our mission or education. After all, how could Mozart compose at three years old? We see prodigies all the time who have no genetic predisposition, so why not believe that they chose to come into families that would benefit from their particular gifts?

This is also the explanation for why some seem to be taken before what we feel is their time. We say, "They went too soon," "They never really got to live," or "It was an accident, and they went too young." Yet their charted time may be entirely different from our own. As simplistic as this sounds, we each have our own allotted time, or "curfew," in each life. Much like when I was in my late teens, midnight was my time to come home, but some of my peers could stay out later.

To show you how conditioned I am, before my dad died, we all took a trip back to Kansas City. I was about 49 years old at the time, and had gone out for the evening with my dear lifelong friend Mary Margaret. It got to be around 11:30, and I told her that I had to get back because my family was staying at a friend's house. At the same time, my father announced to our host that I'd be back by midnight. Everyone laughed and said, "For God's sake, Bill, she's close to 50! Certainly she'll be out later than that."

My dad was adamant. "No, she'll be here."

When Mary Margaret and I drove up at 11:50, Daddy was standing outside with a huge grin. As I walked up to the house, I asked, "Why are you smiling?"

He replied, "I just know you, sweetheart."

This is how it is with our chart: We're programmed to know when we're done. Even if others looking on through their narrow scope see what we didn't fulfill, *we* know that we did all we could—and we have other opportunities to come back and try again.

Some people without any discrimination will pick 10, 25, 40, 50, or more lives—whatever it takes for them to reach their own particular goal of perfection. I've never seen anyone with 100 lives, but I did meet one person who'd lived 99. "Boy," you might say, "they must have been really advanced." Well, they were as advanced as their soul needed to be. Certain individuals just want a high-school education, so to speak, while others want a Ph.D.; but no one on the Other Side looks askance at an individual's level of evolvement. No one carries a badge that proclaims what level they're on or how much better they are—it's only in this hellhole that people are so critically discerning.

Each and every one of our lives is set out in a gigantic pattern. We have the large pattern that encompasses everyone's existence as a whole, and then we have the smaller patterns of each individual life—which is reworked and defined as much as possible to perfect for God. It just makes logical sense that no one can complete everything in one life; if an entity does choose just one, then they have to complete their education by serving as a guide or doing some kind of service on the Other Side. *Everyone* keeps on learning and perfecting until they graduate.

Now, many historians and theologians claim that the concept of reincarnation was brought to light by the Egyptians, but that's not really true. Yes, they contributed in a limited way: They were the first, at least in recorded history, to believe that the soul existed after death—thus the burial chambers filled with food and artifacts that they'd use in the afterlife. Previous to this belief, especially in the ancient Judaic tradition, life after death didn't exist or was unknown. Even Christ's "resurrection" had him coming into flesh.

The real beginning of the belief in reincarnation comes from the ancient East Indian religions, which are also the world's oldest. Their belief in having many lives to perfect the soul was carried over from Lemuria and resides in ancient Sanskrit texts that are thousands of years old. (For more on Lemuria, please see my book *Secrets & Mysteries of the World.*) These texts claim without any complicated dogma that human beings live many lives to fulfill our perfection and to learn our lessons. In other words, one life does not and cannot produce perfection, not only for God but the God within.

Reincarnation as a belief has always been labeled an "Eastern" one; consequently, it wasn't adopted by the Western world and was even suppressed by early Christian leaders. Today, it's estimated that approximately two-thirds of the world believes in reincarnation in one form or another, but it's really only come to the foreground of Western public acknowledgment in the last 20 or 30 years—and is growing in belief as I write these words.

The Gnostics have always believed in reincarnation, but kept silent because they were afraid of being branded heretics. The premise is mentioned frequently in texts such as the Manichaean *Hymn Exhorting the Soul to Remembrance*, from which the following comes: "Remember the cycle of rebirths and the torture of Hell [Earth], where souls are hurt and oppressed. Maintain the fervor of the soul and the treasure of the word, so that you may enter the Paradise of Light."

Gnostic texts such as the Apocrypha, the Nag Hammadi, and the Dead Sea Scrolls; as well as the numerous writings of the Valentinians, Manichaeans, Cathars, and Templars, all support ancient texts about reincarnation. And in Buddhism, the Noble Truth regarding the origin of suffering centers around the thirst to gratify the senses or the cravings for material gains. Too much of this thirst leads to rebirth after rebirth in multiple lives. To reach Nirvana is to attain the level in which you're released from the "rebirth cycle," as well as from the bondage of the endless cycle of birth, death, pain, sorrow, and all the other human conditions of life.

Gnostics don't believe that one can't be comfortable, but think that making only material gain one's entire aim leads to an empty life. Also, Hindus and Buddhists differ from the Gnostics on reincarnation in their unspoken philosophy that humans were sent on this journey to perfect because we weren't good enough to reach God, while Gnostics believe that we choose to come into life to learn and perfect for God with a purpose—not to be just "thrown into it," so to speak.

Reincarnation became a prevalent belief in early Christian dogma thanks to the influence of Greek and Roman thought. St. Gregory, the Bishop of Nyssa, gave words to that effect: "It is absolutely necessary that the soul shall be healed and purified, and if it doesn't take place in one life on Earth, it must be accomplished in future lives." Nevertheless, in A.D. 533, belief in reincarnation was declared a heresy by the Council of Constantinople.

The reason for this was twofold: (1) The Church believed that such a belief detracted from their teachings of death and judgment, which was clearly established in basic Christian doctrine; and (2) the Church believed that it took away a control issue. That is, they realized that if people knew they only had one life in which to make it to the kingdom of heaven, then the Church could exert more control and dictate how people lived their lives. Out of this mentality, stricter dogma came forth that eventually led to the Inquisition. This was also one of the primary reasons behind the Reformation, as rich people were buying indulgences from the Church to assure themselves a place in heaven.

Most Christian churches today don't believe in reincarnation because it conflicts with their dogma of one life, death, and then judgment from God—after all, that's what the Bible says. What they have a hard time explaining, however, is the early deaths of children and the obvious inequities of life that stare that dogma straight in the eye and tear it to shreds. Then they start backpedaling and putting forth exceptions, such as "a child is innocent and can't be judged." Yet a one-life philosophy doesn't begin to explain life's unfairness, and the whole judgment philosophy contradicts an all-loving God. As Huston Smith said in his book *The World's Religions:* "Everything that came from his [Christ's] lips formed the surface of a burning glass to focus human awareness on the two most important facts about life: God's overwhelming love of humanity, and the need for people to accept that love and let it flow through them to others."

I'm constantly amazed at how people can believe that they'll be judged by God, and if found lacking will be thrown into a fiery pit of damnation forever. I'm not condemning their right to believe in any way they want, I'm just astonished that they can swallow that gunk that so many Christian churches put out and believe it. But then, I'm not looking at the economics of the situation—that is, if there's no fear, there won't be any money for more churches.

It's sometimes a sight to behold when you look at the beliefs and values of humankind, along with their inconsistencies. Again, Huston Smith points this out in *The World's Religions* when he writes about how Christ's teachings shocked the populace of his day by giving "hard sayings" that countered the usual prevalent thought and rocked us like an earthquake:

> We are told that we are not to resist evil but to turn the other cheek. The world assumes that evil must be resisted by every means available. We are told to love our enemies and bless those who curse us. The world assumes that friends are to be loved and enemies hated. We are told that the sun rises on the just and the unjust alike. The world considers this undiscriminating; it would like to see clouds over evil people and is offended when they go unpunished. We are told that outcasts and harlots enter the kingdom of God before many who are perfunctorily righteous. Again unfair, the world thinks; respectable people should head the procession. We are told that the gate to salvation is narrow. The world would prefer it to be broad. We are told to be as carefree as birds and flowers. The world counsels prudence. We are told that it is more difficult for the rich to enter the Kingdom than for a camel to pass through a needle's eye. The world admires wealth. We are told that the happy people are those who are meek, who weep, who are merciful and pure in heart. The world assumes that it is the rich, the powerful, and the wellborn who are happy.

Smith then goes on to paraphrase H. G. Wells, who said something to the effect that either there was something mad about Jesus, or our hearts are still too small for his message.

* * *

I'd like to take a moment here to talk about my great-uncle Henry Kaufholz, who died when I was ten. He was Grandma Ada's only brother, and they both inherited their psychic gifts from their mother, who came from Prussian royalty. Henry, who was named after his father, was 6'6", a large blonde, blue-eyed man who was very adventurous with his ability. He even left Springfield, Missouri (where the family settled in after being in Texas), to join the old Florida Chesterfield [Spiritualist] camps.

Uncle Henry was not only a psychic medium, but he also loved to do research—just like me. He was a great proponent of the soul's time line, which I wasn't aware of until my granddaughter pulled out his scrapbook one day. (It's amazing that I've had this bound book all these years and never really read what he'd written.) In it, he talks brilliantly about reincarnation and the allotted time people had . . . and please keep in mind that we're talking about a scrapbook that dates from 1870 to 1912 here.

He states that some of the material was acquired from his grandmother, who was also a psychic and a doctor in Germany (which was quite a feat in those days). The one thing I'm proud of is that those in my family are and were bona-fide, documented psychics—genetic or not. Even Paul, my grandmother's son who died so young, had a spiritual relationship with God that was awe inspiring. The only one that I know about who fell through the cracks was my mother, but that's another story. . . .

My great-uncle never called himself a Gnostic Christian, but the one refrain that runs through his writings is: "Find your own power and your own God-center." He didn't subscribe to any particular organized religion, although he had some background in the Lutheran faith, as many German families did. Grandma Ada, on the other hand, leaned more toward Catholicism and loved Fulton J. Sheen (a great bishop who was very popular on TV in the '50s).

The poetry, letters, and articles that Uncle Henry both wrote and collected are priceless—not just because of their age, but because of when they were written. True, this was the time of Sir Arthur Conan Doyle and Harry Houdini, both of whom were devout researchers of the paranormal, and Spiritualism was enjoying a great revival, especially in Europe—however, it died out as the new century progressed, thanks to the work of so many charlatans.

As I went through these scrapbooks, I noticed Uncle Henry's detailed research on death and dying and the soul's progression through lives. His view was very similar to mine in that he said we all make a contract with God that's completed through many lives. He'd incorporated many articles and essays on the subject, such as the following, which was written in 1912:

> The spiritualistic answers agree as to the revival of the individual after the death of the body, and a mass of evidence is proffered which, in the opinion of all those who have carefully studied it, places the fact of revival beyond dispute. When every possible deduction has been made for fraud, hallucination, [and] self-deception, there remains an irreducible minimum of evidence, which is sufficient to prove that man survives on the other side of death. The evidence, as is well known, is obtained through the class of sensitives known as "mediums," and is of the most varied kinds—writing, materializing under trance conditions, or otherwise.
>
> The greater part of man's consciousness is outside man's physical body, and can manifest itself through the medium of the astral and mental bodies in the astral and mental worlds. In "waking consciousness," the activity is shown through the physical body; but man is not "awake" all the time.
>
> Consciousness is active when the body sleeps, and psychologists have investigated the "dream consciousness," and by the study of dreams, of trance conditions, hypnotic and mesmeric, they have accumulated a number of facts which show when the senses are deadened and the brain is inactive, the consciousness manifests certain powers more extensive than it can show during the use of its ordinary physical apparatus. To put it into other words, the consciousness which works in the waking body is largely withdrawn from the body when it sleeps, and

consciousness is less impeded in the exercise of its powers when it is working outside the dense and comparatively sluggish matter of the physical body.

In certain conditions of very deep trance the consciousness is almost withdrawn from the astral as well as the physical body, and then it works in still rarer regions, and we can have visions of the saints or passed loved ones.

Many an experience of happiness and of suffering are engraven by the consciousness of the spirit's memory [cell memory] and appear as "conscience or knowing" from a subsequent life, as the impulse to do the right and abstain from wrong.

Our future is in our own hands, for the Spirit who is "man" [God] is the inner ruler immortal. We create our future [making our chart] by our present [learning lessons], for we live in a world of law and for him that lives nobly death is but the entrance to a larger consciousness of knowledge and another life.

I included this here because even 100 years ago, people seemed to grasp the meaning of bringing over past memories—and the acknowledgment of cell memory is astounding. Even back then, we had knowledge of it all, and the only thing we lacked was the gigantic statistical findings.

As soon as I read this article, I wondered why it had taken me so long to go through my uncle's book, but then I thought, *How stupid . . . things come when they're supposed to.*

Henry lived to the ripe old age of 96, and his entire life was spent helping people by being a trance medium, and the reason I wanted to talk about him here is partly because he was such a force of spirituality, yet no one really knew about him. I think he deserves some recognition for his great research after almost a century of toiling in a world that was less than sympathetic to his beliefs. Since he was born in the mid-1800s, he must have gone through his own times with skeptics, but from what I heard, nothing bothered him—he persevered even to his death. Until the day he died, he did readings for everyone and anyone, just like my grandmother, and like her, he was also an avid reincarnationist. What's funny is that in the beginning, I wasn't. Oh, I thought it was possible, but truthfully I wasn't going in that direction until I got into hypnosis. It was after many sessions that I finally found irrefutable proof that we live multiple lives; then I went even further to research what we bring over—good *and* bad—from those lives. So through my research, I became a believer.

Today, we're seeing new information come to light in books such as Elaine Pagels's *Gnostic Gospels; The Messianic Legacy* and *Holy Blood, Holy Grail* by Michael Baigent, Richard Leigh, and Henry Lincoln; or Dan Brown's *The Da Vinci Code,* which has become one of the most talked-about books in decades. It's exciting that so much hidden information, which we've been denied for so long, is now coming to light.

How Can This Tenet Help You?

Francine says that I've had 40 lives being psychic (oh, joy). I've also been a Bedouin girl who learned what isolation was like in the desert. When I was an empress, I learned that fame is fleeting; when I was an oracle, I learned how to read for people; and in Atlantis, I learned to write. As a Chinese girl, I learned poverty; in Kenya, I learned to love nature and animals and the pureness of human life; and in Poland, I learned how to care for my sick loved ones. I've learned to be without children, to be humbled, elated, poor, rich, sick, rejected, and on and on it goes. Each of my lives built on the next and taught me different things . . . and so it is with you.

Just as I was never a baby killer or a tyrant, neither were you. You're not dark or you wouldn't care about finding truth (even if you were curious). So, if you can release ills and phobias—which I've done—by talking to the soul mind and releasing the carryover from a past life, how can that be just a healing story? The mind is too clever to be fooled by some tale that doesn't ring true to the soul.

I'm also convinced (after obsessing about the fact that I can't see more than about 100 years from now) that it's absolutely true that humankind only has that much time left on this planet. It was right in front of me, yet I didn't see it. How many times have I said that I've never seen so many people who are on their last lives—*duh!* On that last life, which many of us are already living, we'll go through all of these experiences and many more to make our souls strong. We may not like it—like me, we can sometimes gripe and bitch through it—but we'll get up, dust ourselves off, and keep on going.

Now while I'm sure that the final days are coming, I'm not like all those soothsayers who have predicted doom—I'm just convinced that after millions of years on this planet, in which we've learned through many lifetimes for God, this schematic will end.

Don't worry, though—there will be other plans for us: We'll either stay on the Other Side and learn, or we'll wait for another planet to swing into place and possibly explore life there. Regardless, life will never end, but I can assure you that nothing *anywhere* will be like it's been here. I'm convinced that that's why our Lord and the other messengers came here—to try to nurture a truly hellish planet. Tragically, every time they did, they were punished for it.

Even Martin Luther, the founder of the Lutheran Church who tried to bring about love and peace and quell corruption, was branded a heretic. His whole stance was that the scriptures didn't support much of the politics of the Church at that time—in much the same way that human-made doctrine ruled out the reincarnation that was in the original books because they felt it took away from Christianity.

I've always wondered how a merciful and all-loving God wouldn't give us as many tries as we needed for our own souls to live and advance. Yet if anyone tries to bring the reality of hope, logic, and love to the table, they're condemned because they don't fear God or get caught up in a devil (which, as we know, doesn't exist anyway). Much of the dogma in Christianity today is such that you sit back and wonder, *Where did that church law come from?* Humans, that's who!

No matter if you believe in one life or many, be assured that God is all-knowing, forever loves you, and will never abandon you. After all, if Jesus promised that he would be with us always, why wouldn't his Father do likewise through our life-after-life journeys? As Christ said in Matthew 5:45–48: "So that you may be children of your Father in heaven; for he makes his sun rise on the evil and on the good, and sends rain on the righteous and the unrighteous. . . . Be perfect, therefore, as your heavenly father is perfect."

* * * * * *

TENET XVI

Devote your life, your soul, your very existence, to the service of God. For only there will you find meaning in life.

I've shared what this tenet relates in many ways over the years, but sometimes people are confused as to how they should really devote their lives to God. They think that they have to be saintly, when the truth is that most of us already have the calling to live the best we can. And I'm not trying to be pessimistic when I say that so many people are enduring lives of quiet desperation or futility, are in a desert period, or are just surviving—and they don't realize that this, too, can be a glory to God.

Think about it—if life wasn't hard, we wouldn't learn. After all, we can't master algebra if we're not subjected to its equations. The worst thing we can do, however, is despair and go into apathetic thinking, such as, *What difference can I make? I'm only one person.* Unfortunately, because of the way the world is, we're going to feel overwhelmed—that's just the way it is—but that's no reason for giving up either.

So many times in readings, people are worried that they're not on track, that God won't forgive or is mad at them, or that they haven't done enough to perfect. None of us should be worrying about these things—as I've said so often, individuals who are bad or dark don't care—and I'd like to see us all become more optimistic instead of constantly dwelling on pain and suffering.

I don't talk to, or do readings for, too many happy people, so a lot of folks ask me, "How do you, your son, and your staff stay positive with all the pain and suffering you hear?" Well, it comes down to the belief that God is good and we're here to learn. It's true that, like a doctor, I don't tend to see well people, but I try to give truth and help or even help make their pain stop.

This reminds me of a beautiful meditative prayer I once read, called "Enlightened Buddha":

> *Beyond the beliefs of any one religion,*
> *there is truth of the human spirit.*
> *Beyond the power of nations, there*
> *is the power of the human heart.*
> *Beyond the ordinary mind, the*
> *power of wisdom, love, and healing*
> *energy are at work in the universe.*
> *When we find peace within our hearts,*
> *we contact these universal powers.*
> *This is our only hope.*

In all the major religions, the basic themes of love, giving, and peace are pervasive. So if we go through life as the various messengers have told us to, then we've devoted our existence to the service of God. It's as simple as that.

So many times we note the lives of the saints, clerics, and holy people; along with the Gandhis, Mother Teresas, and Martin Luther Kings of this world; and we feel inferior compared to what they've sacrificed and accomplished because they really seem to have lived their lives totally for

God. Well, we don't have to be canonized or written up in history books—it's what we do in our everyday lives that puts notches in our spiritual belt.

My guide Francine also says that *everyone* has had a life in which they worked and gained some noteworthy spiritual knowledge—but not every person who gave up their lives to work tirelessly for a spiritual movement got headlines. After all, we didn't always have TV and newspapers to follow every human-interest story. Take Mohammed, Buddha, and Jesus, for example: Who interviewed them? Who would have known about my grandmother, who died in 1954, if it weren't for me? Yes, there are a few people in Kansas City who remember her, but if I hadn't written about her, who would know?

It's our actions that change our circle of influence and impact the world. So when we feel that what we've done isn't enough, we just need to remember that our lights are in heaven, and angels are writing down our deeds in golden script in their scrolls. (Many times it's actually *better* to do our good works in comparative obscurity.)

Devoting our lives to God and our own family and friends, and just treating others as we want to be treated is so simple and so wonderful. Yet we can oftentimes take this too far and get too scrupulous. We become afraid that if we have negative thoughts, get angry, lash out or get cranky at a loved one, speak sarcastically to a grocery clerk, or what have you, then that means we aren't living a life devoted to God and good works. Well, take comfort—these are stress-related *human* emotions, and we've got to allow ourselves to be human. Personally, I don't trust people who are too goody-goody and thus never stand up for themselves.

For more than 30 years, I've told my staff to always be courteous, but they're not on the phone to put up with someone who's rude or insulting. The customer is always right when they have an honest and courteous complaint . . . however, I remember that we had this guy who used to call at least once a week and berate anyone who answered

the phone. He'd say things like, "You people are all pho-
nies—you just want money, and you're all a bunch of scam
artists."

I happened to be walking through the office one day
and heard Michael (my secretary of 18 years) saying, "I'm
sorry you feel this way, sir, but I can assure you that we're
accredited and never entrap anyone. No one is forced to call
us, and we don't solicit anyone."

I asked Pam, who's been with me for 30 years, "What's
this about?"

Warily, she said, "It's just some guy who calls once a
week and reads us the riot act."

I marched in there and took the phone out of Michael's
hand. "Who is this?" I asked the caller, knowing already
that his name was Richard.

He responded, "Is this Sylvia?"

I said, "Yes, it is, and I'd like to hear your complaints!"

He stammered that he thought we were in the business for the money, and I replied, "You're right, we *do* need
money because we have ministers and an office staff of 22,
overhead, a phone bill that would floor most people, Workers' Comp, taxes, and leased computers and office equip-
ment." Then, as if it mattered, I continued, "And as for me,
I'm on salary, I don't own a house, and I lease my car." I
wondered why I was going through this with a clearly ignorant person, so I ended the conversation with, "Apparently
you have too much time on your hands, and if you call back
here again, no one will be allowed to talk to you."

There was a long pause, and then I heard, "I'm sorry, I
didn't know."

Remember that before you go into a fight, you should
at least go in with knowledge. As I told this Richard, "If you
didn't know," I replied, "then you don't need to spread your
hateful accusations."

He called back a week later to apologize again, and he
even sent us flowers.

Now I'm not telling you this story to be a martyr, because

I do live very well. I have a nice home, a great Ford van, a wonderful family, and plenty to eat—but I think that we all get too tied into what our economic status is. It's true that the economy goes up and down nationwide; while individually it seems that if people have money they're afraid they're going to lose it, and if they don't have it, they're afraid they'll end up homeless. I'm not saying that these aren't valid concerns, but if we shove down our expectations and also believe that God will take care of us, then we'll realize that we don't need very much to exist happily. We collect (I should talk) and hold on to everything (even what we don't need), but we forget that everything is temporary—after all, we won't be taking anything with us when we go Home.

I've been bankrupt, and also well provided for—and either way, I truly was fine as long as I could provide shelter for my family and put food on the table. But worries such as these, as authentic as we think they are, keep spirituality away. God always provides a way, and sometimes the small things in life—like a "Thank you," a smile, or a meant compliment—are what really count.

My youngest son is like me when it comes to animals, and he has three cats that just show up at his house. A friend was sitting at his table, saw Chris go get food for each of the cats, and asked, "Why would you do that?"

"Because they're hungry," my son replied. It's as simple as that: If there's a need, fill it. We should never turn our backs on a need. For example, I was in Wal-Mart one day when my grandson Willy pointed out an old lady trying to reach a roll of paper towels. I went over and got it down for her. People were walking by in throngs, and no one but a child noticed her plight.

I really don't believe that people are mean; rather, we've all become so focused on our own problems that we really don't see the big picture. It's like we have blinders on and all we see is the road ahead—that is, getting from point A to point B. Time not only flies but seems to be speeding up, and we never seem to have time for anything. We fill our days with useless tasks that will not only wait, but many times won't matter if they ever get done. "If I don't get to that sale today, I'll miss it!" we worry. So we rush around to *not* miss it, and what does that get us? Couldn't we live without it?

I don't mean that we shouldn't enjoy the simple pleasures of life, but all these have-tos are getting to be too much. I mean, lunch *has* to be at noon, dinner at six, and bed at ten (or whatever). We have so many rituals and rules: Monday is wash day, Tuesday is housecleaning day, and so forth. Everything can wait for us, so we really need to try to change our regimen if it's so demanding. As I've mentioned, during my first marriage it was almost as if I had obsessive-compulsive disorder—I was cleaning, scrubbing, cooking, working, and going to school to fill up my outside life so that I wouldn't have to think of what I was missing on the inside.

I was so proud of myself at Christmas last year when I had people over. My table holds 8 but there were 20 people, so the kids and I ate at the coffee table. My granddaughter, Angelia, lit every candle in the house, and there were drippings everywhere. For a moment I got a little crazy, and then I told myself, *Who cares, considering the joy it brought her? What's a little wax, Sylvia?*

Yes, I like cleanliness, but a home is a home and not a showplace. I remember years ago when my first husband and I went to visit a friend. Kansas City is cold in the winter, yet this woman had everything covered with plastic and there were floor runners everywhere. Coming in from the cold, the plastic stuck to me as if I had static electricity, and it was freezing. All I could think of was how long it must have taken her to cover everything in this plastic house.

You see, we get sidetracked by things that don't last anyway, when our time would be better spent performing a good deed, educating ourselves, or even sending a remote healing to someone. However, austerity isn't the way to go either—to spend ten hours in meditation is fine, but it's all inside you and won't help your fellow humans.

We don't have to spend lots of time doing a *great* act of good; just something small at least once a day, such as a telephone call, a card, or a visit; letting someone get ahead of us in line at a store; or just giving a stranger a smile or a kind word can do wonders for a heavy heart. I remember when I was ten years old, for instance, and I attended early mass every day. I'd be there in the pew before my classmates arrived, and there was an old woman who would come in. She always walked by me, and I always smiled at her.

One day after about a year, she walked over to me and said, "Sweet girl, I love coming to church, but what I treasure is your sweet smile—it brightens my whole day. I hope you never lose it." What seemed natural to me was a bonus to a lonely old lady, and from then on, I never forgot that the smallest kindnesses are sometimes the real gems in life to a soul that thirsts to be recognized or loved.

I don't want to bore you with my Uncle Henry's writings and collections, but this fits so well here. It's called "The Brighter Side."

> *Someone committed murder last night.*
> *But hundreds of thousands were kind,*
> *For the wrong that is done is forever in sight*
> *To the good that are fearfully blind.*
>
> *Someone deserted his children today,*
> *But millions of fathers are true.*
> *The bad deeds are not such a fearful array*
> *Compared to the good that men do.*
>
> *Somebody stole from his brother last night,*
> *But millions of honest men live.*
> *Someone was killed in a murderous fight,*
> *But thousands were glad to forgive . . .*

Their brothers, the wrongs that were fancied or real.
The crimes that we hear of each day
Compared in the good deeds that we could reveal,
Make not such a fearful array.

I would answer the men who stand up and declare,
That the world is much given to vice.
That the sum of men's crimes every day, everywhere,
Can't compare with man's sweet sacrifice.

That for every black soul there are thousands pure white.
The sum of the sinners hopefully is few,
And I know in my heart that the world is all right,
When I think of the good that hopefully men do.

This is a beautiful and optimistic view of humankind, and it's true that we can steep ourselves in all the bad and never see the good that people do. Yes, I know the world is full of stress, with wars and famine and natural disasters, but we'll survive. And if we don't, what's the worst thing that could happen? We'll all go Home to God together.

It amazes me how many times I've talked to people who've tried to commit suicide and failed, but if you tell them that they have a health problem, they freak out. It all comes down to control: We say, "I want to be in charge of my life, my finances, my family, and my destiny." Well, when will we realize that we're not in control down here? We've made our chart and it's set, so we can choose to live it with dignity or sorrow.

Again, in order to enjoy our very existence, we just need to take one day at a time—enjoy the simple pleasures and quit anticipating what could be or was. If we live as if we have a limited time here on Earth (which, of course, we all have), then we can stand before God and say that we did our best in our existence for Him/Her.

How Can This Tenet Help You?

How many times a day do you think about God? If you don't do so regularly, try to keep Him/Her in your mind. In almost any situation you can ask yourself, "What would our Lord do?" It's easy once you start (we certainly obsess enough about everything else). Just to say affirmations such as "God loves me, and I am full of grace" does wonders for your soul. You can also follow up by saying, "Whatever I go through, You will never abandon me."

Even if you live to be 100 years old, this life is short and transient—it's merely a place to visit and make different, not unlike those who go to Bosnia, Rwanda, or other such places to help others. Now you don't have to join the Peace Corps (although this is truly admirable), but you can certainly go the extra mile to help others in your circle. Sometimes when I'm tired and someone calls me for assistance, I force myself to take the call—and by the time I've helped them, I'm rejuvenated.

I'm reminded of this woman who phoned me the other day, moaning about losing her faith—she felt alone, useless, and abandoned. Yes, we all feel that way at one time or another, but hopefully we don't let despair immobilize us. I said, "I don't have a magic potion to get you out of this," but she wanted some advice anyway. I said, "Just get out and take a class, join a church, or even pray."

"But I'm too tired to do anything," she replied.

"You're depressed because it's all about 'poor you,'" I countered. "You need to get past that. The best way is to volunteer, perhaps at a hospital."

One month later she wrote to say that she was helping out at a hospice and felt better than she ever had. I know that to get out of the hole of despair—hell, to even get dressed and go out some days—is hard, but it isn't as hard as living in the nothingness of your own pains and ills. The old expression that there are always people worse off than you are doesn't work when you feel like hell, but no one can get you out but you.

If you look at life as a trip to complete your mission for God and yourself, so many of these worries go away. Then, as I've said, your existence will mean something. You'll be setting an example for others, which will make your mind, your soul, and even your physical self better. Try to find happy people, because negativity is catching and it's like a terrible flu of the soul. If someone drains you and is always complaining and depressed, get away!

Time may be running out for this negative world, but that doesn't mean that there isn't time to raise its spiritual consciousness. So, regardless of what your lot in life might be, you still can stop and give someone a smile, a shoulder to cry on, or a helping hand to get them through the desert. I promise that no matter how down, tired, or ill you feel, if you give of yourself, God will take care of you (plus, too much of your own self is probably what's making you feel so down).

I know that there's a universal law in which God says, "If you take care of mine, I'll take care of you." Try it like I have, and you'll be living proof that it works.

※ ※ ※ ※ ※ ※

TENET XVII

War is profane; defense is compulsory.

We Gnostics do not believe in war, for through the ages it hasn't accomplished much except death and destruction. We do believe that we must protect our lives and homes, but to have most of the world in turmoil is ridiculous. Look at all the battles that we know of through-out history and how useless they were—and the reasons for them often boil down to greed and power. Of course we need defense to protect our loved ones, but there are so many senseless skirmishes over land, the acquisition of power, or conquering others. For example:

— The Crusades started out to be a holy war to take back Jerusalem from the Moors, but they quickly turned into exercises in ravaging and pillaging. So what started out as a noble cause turned to avarice and greed . . . along with the accompanying bloodshed.

— America had a revolutionary war in order to be freed from the strict English rule, but what I find so ironic is that the colonists put far more religious restrictions on themselves (and others) than they'd suffered in England. In addition, we wanted freedom and fought a war to get it—and then turned around and subjected other people to slavery. It's funny how so many times we become what we fight against.

— Adolf Hitler was a maniacal man who fancied himself to be a demigod and attacked countries just so he could conquer and enslave them. Of course he should have been stopped for his atrocities against the Judaic people and others—defense was mandatory. But even today, there are still pockets of people who admire him and believe that the Aryan race is superior.

— None of us will ever know (at least I won't) what the Vietnam War was about. Not only that, but we so shamefully treated the brave people who served in that waste of human life!

From the beginning of time, humankind seems to have used war as their mode to fix whatever wrongs they think exist. Now when we look at Sanskrit texts that are thousands of years old, which describe war and devastation from flying machines; the Romans, Genghis Khan, Alexander the Great, Napoleon, Attila the Hun, and other conquerors; or the marauding Celts and other tribes, it appears that humans have always waged war on each other. In the process, civilizations have disappeared and precious legacies such as the libraries at Alexandria (which contained irreplaceable ancient scrolls and books of human history) have been lost forever. That's the ultimate tragedy of war: It destroys so much of our civilization's art, writings, and buildings, which can never ever be replaced—not to mention the most precious things of all: human lives.

War always seems to start out with a higher purpose, but remember that "he who lives by the sword, dies by the sword." Proponents like to trot out the law of cause and effect, which seems to be more powerful than what we think of as karma. In other words, for every action there will be a reaction that many times has a rebound effect. Yet the motive for war never seems to stay so pure.

To stop the tyranny that threatens our existence is one thing, but to have war just for the sake of conquering and pillaging is morally, spiritually, and ethically wrong. It's like mob violence in that it becomes a senseless trigger effect that leads to the raping and killing of women and the torture and crucifixion of those who don't share the "right" beliefs.

America is a prime example of this. Our country started out with high hopes and a motive to provide freedom for everyone. But we proceeded to take over land that belonged to the Indians, and then relegated them to desert and swampland areas that nobody wanted (which we called "reservations"). Of course when we found something valuable on the reservations, such as gold in the Black Hills of South Dakota, we moved the tribes to even bleaker places.

Americans have murdered, lynched, and debased others; taken over lands that weren't rightfully ours; and gone to Africa to acquire slaves. Why? To make the local gentry feel superior? Because we're lazy? Or to show how well off certain landowners were because they could keep slaves? This was all just a by-product of the greed and power that causes humans to wage war on other humans. Conquering and enslaving has always been about money and power.

Humankind has always been its own worst enemy. The problem lies in not believing in our inner spirituality—so we become so frightened or so controlled by emotion that all intellect goes out the window. Look how Hitler took hold in Germany: It became a mass frenzy for all the wrong reasons (even though they might have seemed noble at the onset), and then the whole thing disintegrated into giving a tyrant too much religious, political, and monetary power, and it affected millions.

Humankind must—and cannot wait any longer to—try to get along. I truly believe that we don't have much time left on this planet to learn for God, so we've got to live together in harmony and not worry about who has what land and who has the most resources. We have to stop the discriminations in this world that are racial, ethnic, sexual, religious, or political . . . after all, we're all made by the same God.

Yes, we Gnostics do believe in defending our country, homes, and loved ones, but we've never been for war for war's sake. When I formed Novus Spiritus, I put us under "conscientious objector" status, with the caveat that if our country was attacked, we'd help to defend it.

True Christians don't believe in starting a fight. The best thing we can do is strive for peace, since the negativity of war just begets more negativity. Now you may wonder, "Don't you want to help others, save the world, and bring about freedom and democracy?" Of course I do! I believe that we should make our voices heard over excessive taxation, inequities, and the like, but in the last 65 years we've had one war after the other.

I remember in the 1940s when they had blackouts and air-raid drills (my dad was an air-raid warden). I was at an age where I thought this was exciting, since my grandmother and I would sit in the dark and listen to the shortwave radio. Later, when it dawned on me how many lives were lost, it really tore me up. It was then that I realized that, regardless of what goes on in the world, we must all strive for peace.

I want to make a very important point here: *In no way am I trying to imply that I don't support our men and women who fight on orders from our government.* It's just that, as I've said for years, after living through World War II—along with the combat in Korea, Vietnam, Kuwait, and Iraq—I strongly feel that we should think about protecting and taking care of our own country first. Even the Bible says that charity begins at home. If everyone kept peace in their own dwellings, their own blocks, their own communities, and their own countries, then we'd certainly cut down on the dissent in the world.

Acts of war have never stopped and are still prevalent today for the same old-as-time reasons. Sometimes they're even infantile in their messages of "If you hurt me, I'll hurt you" or "I want your riches, your women, your slaves, and your land so that I can conquer and feel powerful." Battles fought for these reasons are always futile and useless, for all "empires" crumble eventually under poor rule.

We can even see this in a microcosm of an office or corporation. Take Enron, for instance—the corruption became overwhelming because of greed. What the company's executives did used to be called "cooking the books"; in this case, they put out false income reports that made their stock jump in price, while the CEOs were making themselves rich with stock options and selling them off. Yet when the end came, thousands of hardworking employees were left with a useless and overpriced stock, and the company was basically bankrupt.

In this country, we've seen junk-bond dealers, bad stocks, real estate that went up and then crashed down, and the bursting of the dot-com bubble—all of which has wreaked financial havoc on many. We're currently in a time when we have to tighten our belts and be vigilant about our finances. It's sad but true, but as the world gets greedier, we have to become more careful. That doesn't mean we need to live in a fortress, but being smart and aware has to be our focus now.

* * *

I find it strange that our own homes can become mini war zones. For example, we choose sides; often vie for the affection and attention of one or more members; and experience jealousy, vengeance, and greed. I remember when my second husband's mother died and we went over to see his stepfather. When I walked in, I was appalled: The poor man was sitting in a vacant house—all that was left was a chair, a bed, a TV, and two lamps. My husband's three brothers and their families had descended like locusts before their mother was even cold in the grave, and they'd taken almost all the furniture, dishes, glassware, jewelry, and anything else that wasn't nailed down.

The stepfather was obviously grief-stricken and in shock, yet he looked at me and said, "Mom wanted you to have some of her jewelry, but I don't know where it is."

"That's all right," I assured him. "Don't you worry—I don't need anything because I have my memories of her." (Everyone as a precaution should draft an airtight will, but even then families can become torn apart.)

The other problem that causes so much friction in our lives, whether it's personally, socially, religiously, or politically, is not telling the truth. The problem (or maybe it's a good thing) is that lies always unravel. The lust for power and money can certainly cause trouble, but lies can also insidiously wreck families, for children learn to duplicate this behavior. And no matter how much the populace pleads for truth, governments or heads of state keep on lying. They tell us, "Taxes will go down" (they don't), "There will be work for all" (there isn't), "We want peace" (as they invade another country), and on and on. We see it in our personal lives, too, when our loved ones say, "I won't drink anymore" (they do), "I'll stop spending our money" (they don't), or "I won't ever be unfaithful" (they are), and so on.

If we can't trust our country, our beliefs, or our loved ones, then our life will feel as if it has derailed. We must be vigilant so that we can keep war out of our homes by demanding honesty, loyalty, and commitment (which is our Gnostic motto), because if we have these three, everything else falls into place.

However, we must be aware of the war we often wage

within *ourselves*. In fact, we are the most dangerous adversary we can face. To illustrate, I'd like to share something I wrote in my old Douay Bible in August 1954. I'd forgotten all about these words until I happened to open right to them as I was doing research for this book. Although what I wrote is quite personal, I'm going to share it with you because it's so pertinent to our "inner wars."

> This night, dear God, things have fallen into place, out of my confused and bewildered mind I realize. Things for so long have been chaos, and now I feel I know the answer. I have tried to figure out my life and chart and even lean on others, when it should have just simply been You all the time.
>
> Far have I traveled from Thee, O God, and long were the years I traveled with Thee—happy in your light—and then life and work and time filled in and I no longer turned to You. My faith and beliefs went begging, as if they drifted to a foreign shore. Now this day, kneeling, I saw what I hadn't seen for months . . . a light and a voice in my heart. "I am still here . . . you have only to turn inward and look." And I did and my whole life became clear. The decisions I must make, and the road I must follow—it is all so easy now, when before, when I was so outward it was so hard. How could I have crowded in so many things before You—when for so long I lived so near You? You are my true love, and the answer to all frustrations . . . a complete and perfect outlet. The only Being that never falters or fails. O God, I'm home again and so at peace and so much more in harmony with my public destiny and what You want from me. This road that I have chosen will not be as fearful and lonely as I imagine . . . for You above shall be with me all through my life showing me the way.

This was a plaintive plea—a recognition of a war going on inside of me—that I wrote when I realized that I really had to go public. It has been hard, but never lonely . . . and neither will your road be if you keep peace in your heart, your home, and your community.

How Can This Tenet Help You?

My grandmother used to say, "If you weed your own garden, you won't have to worry, and you're also keeping the weeds' spores from other people's gardens." It's like I've said so often: Take care of your home first, and *then* go out and help others. In other words, don't go next door and feed your neighbor's children if yours are starving—sharing is better.

It can be difficult to have this philosophy when our global community has suffered so much recently. In just a few short years, we've seen the tsunami that struck Indonesia, Sri Lanka, and India; earthquakes in Mexico, Japan, and Turkey; volcanic eruptions, floods, and tornados; and hurricanes that destroyed so much of the South—it's almost as if Mother Nature is declaring war on us for what we've done to her. On top of all this, we've lived through the bombing of the federal building in Oklahoma and trains in Madrid and London, the attacks on the World Trade Center and the Pentagon, and the mailing of anthrax—all the work of terrorists. Then we've had to deal with SARS, AIDS, and various types of new flu epidemics that are real biological wars, which have medical technology faltering in the onslaught of the resurgence of illnesses thought to be conquered and new ones that have no cure as yet.

When you look at this big picture, don't your daily worries seem insignificant? If you do what you can for humanity as a whole by giving aid to those who need you and praying that the world will become more spiritual, you'll be elevated above your personal times of stress and strife.

The mother who loses her son to war might be inconsolable in her loss. Yet if she knows that he died for a greater good, then his moral and spiritual intention to make this world a better place will rub off on her. No death is useless, but many times they seem to be senseless. But bless the many young men and women who go to all corners of the earth from Germany to Korea, Vietnam to Iraq, following the life charts they created in order to help make this a better world.

I didn't want my sons to go to war, and I was fortunate that when they came of age, there was no draft. But now my grandsons are growing up, and there doesn't seem to be an end in sight. I'm certain that if we stop these wars, our consciousness and spirituality will be raised and *every* parent's child will be safe. So let's lift our love and spirituality to create a conversion to peace throughout the world, and there will be no more sacrifices of life.

When I was a little girl, we could walk anywhere at any time and no harm would befall us; also, no one locked their doors. But the world pendulum swings wildly, and most of us cannot do that anymore. The good news is that once it swings to the bad, it always goes to a neutral place and then comes back to a better place. Before the end of times, we're going to see peace. In fact, I'm convinced that extraterrestrials will show themselves in the next decade to help us bring peace to this world. We need *some* type of intervention, since we don't seem to be able to do it ourselves. However, each and every one of us still has the power of our God-centeredness to not only pray for peace, but to also ask for God's army of angels to surround this planet.

Any concept that's not built on spiritual motives will come crashing down like a house of cards. If something doesn't feel right—even a cause that seems just, but begins to be run by ego—run! To go and live in a compound and eat rice and give all your money to one person who promises salvation is illogical. This is what gives use to the often believed anti-Christ, which won't be one person, but a type of insane ideology that will sweep across the world. We still have years to create a type of harmonious convergence to fight this movement and lift the energy of a sick world.

In fact, Francine says that in the last two decades, angels have surrounded the earth more than ever before. You may wonder why there's been so much horror then, and all I can say is, "Can you even comprehend how bad it would be if they *weren't* here?"

It's like the e-mails I received after 9/11 in which countless people told me about all the angels that were spotted in the sky. And look at how people pulled together in that crisis—I saw more patriotism than I've ever seen in my lifetime, then it sort of dwindled away. Regardless, what we face now or in the future was not only planned in our charts, but the real strength will be reveled in how we handle these situations.

That's why it's so important to raise your spirituality by never forgetting to surround yourself and your loved ones with the white light of the Holy Spirit. And if you keep saying positive affirmations, you can prevent many negative occurrences. Stopping war and creating peace will engender miracles for all of humankind.

✳ ✳ ✳ ✳ ✳ ✳

TENET XVIII

Death is the act of returning Home;
it should be done with grace and dignity.
You may preserve that dignity by refusing
prolonged use of artificial life-support
systems. Let God's will be done.

Human beings, either on their own, or as a result of their religious or spiritual beliefs, seem to either fear death or feel that dying for a cause is noble. And besides love, there's no other subject that's been debated, argued, or eulogized more: "For the wages of sin is death," "Death comes like a thief in the night," "The angel of death has come for you," and on and on. The subject has permeated our poetry and art, along with our social, religious, and commercial sectors.

For many years, death has been viewed as the ultimate punishment for humankind. Consequently, all types of religious doctrine have grown out of trying to escape it or learning to fear it as the ultimate end and not the beginning. The macabre saying "ashes to ashes, dust to dust" has always seemed like such a depressing lie to me because it sounds as if we came from nothing and will go back to nothing . . . which, of course, couldn't be further from the truth.

Death has been around me all my life. I was introduced to it with my grandfather's passing when I was three years old. Later on came the deaths of my grandmother and my Uncle Marcus, and even my own near-death experience at 26. But I think that the passing of my grandmother's son Paul, which happened long before I was born, may have actually impacted me the most. A very spiritual mystic, Paul told my mother before he died that she'd have a daughter with "the gift," and he asked that she call the baby Sylvia, after his favorite song.

Below is an excerpt from the eulogy that Bishop Robert Nelson Spencer gave at Paul's funeral on January 4, 1931, (five years before my birth). I've included it because it's a beautiful tribute, and I'm also very proud of the spirituality that came from those who went before me. Perhaps it will also give you insight into what began to shape my life and chart.

> Paul [Coil] did not grow up like his great namesake, the apostle, with frail stature and some mysterious physical defect . . . this Paul grew up [so] like a straight young tree that I have not seen a finer specimen of young manhood than was his. When he was in high school, he swept everything before him in the games and on the track. And for that they gave him a scholarship to the local college.
>
> But Paul Coil had something besides strength in that fine young body—in his throat, there was a golden voice. And Paul valued that gift of song more than he valued the pole vault or the broad jump. So Paul went to the School of Fine Arts at [the University of Kansas in] Lawrence rather than to the local college. Later Paul took that lovely tenor voice of his down through the Southwest, singing in competition on the radio, and there would have been a good contract for Paul to sign if he had lived. For it is true of Paul, as it was of another:

Because I have loved so vainly,
And have sung with such faltering breath,
The Master in mercy gave me
The beautiful boon of Death.

I have always held that of those separating things, written of in the Eighth of Romans—and it was Paul's namesake who wrote them—that of "life and death and principalities and powers," the most separating thing is life. It was life that separated Paul and me. I did not know until the deadly sarcoma had laid that fine young athlete on his bed that he was in Kansas City. I did not know that he had come, when he could get away from his own choir, with the crowds to Grace and Holy Trinity; that he had knelt there when it must have been an agony with that poor afflicted leg of his. . . .

In one respect he was like that other Paul, after whom he was named: Paul Coil was a missionary. He did not go up and down Asia and the half of Europe when society was pagan to the core, but he did move through a society that still has many pagan ideas, and his fine face and fine eyes and handsome young body gave him something of that appeal that has made paganism in every age turn and look. Perhaps the most remarkable thing about Paul Coil was the testimony that came to his mother when he was dead . . . [people called her] and said: "His natural and unaffected goodness changed my life." That is why I am writing about Paul. I think it is worthwhile to write about Paul Coil the missionary!

So vital and clean had been that young manhood that Paul was long to die. Even the doctors in St. Luke's marveled at his hold on life. Again and again I went to see him, thinking it must be time to close those great dark eyes, but there was always in them hope—his hope to live and get well—and never any fear at all.

I saw him last in the evening of his last day. He put up two very thin hands, clasping one of mine. "I am glad to see you, Bishop, but I am very tired tonight . . . I guess I am sleepy, Bishop—won't you wake me up?" And in the wee hours of the morning, God wakened Paul from the dream of life.

Of all the eulogies I've heard Bishop Spencer give, this is one of the best. I also came to love this man who confirmed me in the Episcopalian religion (I later became Catholic), and I loved the way *he* loved God in a deep, poetic way. He believed, long before most people started putting it forth, that death was a celebration of life.

Just as my Uncle Paul did, most individuals know when their time is coming. And if they're aware, the people around them can feel their loved one almost "retract," or pull their soul away. (For example, I saw my father and some of my friends do this.)

Even in the deaths of children or trauma victims, a loved one will many times report, "He said that he wasn't going to live long." For example, a woman I talked to recently said that her granddaughter had told the family that she wanted to be with her grandfather (who'd died a year previously), and he'd even come for her twice. The granddaughter said, "The third time, I'll go." And she did.

Now, I can feel when someone is not only sick, but just gives up. Life just gets too tiring—or their chart says that it's time to graduate. When the brother of Gina, my son Chris's wife at the time, died, it was such a terrible tragedy. He was an incredibly sweet and unassuming young man—kind, caring, and considerate—and he was only in his 20s. He'd had terrible headaches all his life and had started to have seizures, so they had to operate.

Well, we all decided to throw a party for him on the evening before he was to go into the hospital. He had the best time that night—he even came up to me to tell me how much fun he was having. Unfortunately, the surgery came and there was no hope of recovery. I was outside with my granddaughter, Angelia, while the family was with Gina's brother (his name was also Chris). All of a sudden, young Chris appeared to me and said, "Please tell them that I'm all right and they can quit rubbing me. I'm going to play my guitar and have a lot of fun now."

Just then, Gina came down, and I told her what had happened. Sure enough, she said that the nurses were indeed rubbing her brother, and the doctor had confirmed that it was hopeless. Soon after, we held a memorial service for this wonderful young man, who will always be remembered in our hearts as a gentle soul who loved everyone and was loved *by* everyone.

Gina and Chris's mother, Phyllis, will never get over this (who can or does?), but the family has survived and gone on bravely. As a tribute to him, they donated many of his organs after his death, which helped six people to either live or improve their quality of life. As I said at the time, "He did go happy and positively—it's only those of us left behind who are suffering from the loss."

With all the grief I've felt for the people I've loved and lost, I've *never* demanded external means just to keep them alive when their quality of life is gone. When my father was 87 and full of cancer, they wanted him to be on life support. He begged me to have them give him morphine for his pain, yet the doctor told me, "We don't want him to get addicted."

"Huh?!" I retorted. "He's dying, so turn up the drip." I mean, my dad certainly wasn't going to get up and go dancing! Of course it was hard to witness this, but I couldn't stand to see him suffer, no matter how much I wanted him to stay with me.

Medicine is marvelous, but sometimes we keep people alive when there's no *life* left. Yes, miracles happen, but for the terminally ill and the elderly, we need to let God's will be done. We'd all be wise to sign the "Do Not Resuscitate" form, or if we experience brain damage, we'll be on a machine for years while our soul has already vacated our body. (I discussed this subject in detail, especially as it pertained to the Terri Schiavo case, not too long ago in one of my newsletters.)

We spend so much time celebrating a soul coming in, but if he or she is going Home, we don't want to face it. Don't get me wrong, because I've been there—I know this is horribly hard, but the spiritual and unselfish thing to do is to talk the person over to the Other Side. My second husband, Dal, was able to do this for his mother when she lay in a coma due to lymphatic cancer. He related how he spoke in her left ear (which is controlled by the intellect) and explained that she should look for and go toward the white light, and then she'd meet a loved one who would help and go with her to the Other Side.

Dal then told me that he sat back in a chair by her bedside, and within moments he saw his mother come out of her body, as an entity from the Other Side came to stand beside her. He said that they stood there for a few minutes and then proceeded to move away and disappear through a wall. He was so moved by the incident, and the fact that he was able to help his mother pass peacefully. (At the time of her passing, I felt her go, too—moments later Francine confirmed that my dear mother-in-law had passed over and was getting ready to attend a big homecoming party.)

Every one of our Novus Spiritus ministers who has died went peacefully without fear or hesitation. Of course we Gnostics fight for life, but when the time comes, we can just let go with dignity and smile with joy because we're going Home to our loved ones, Jesus, and our blessed Mother and Father God. For us, death is a celebration of life—but now it's over, and we've graduated.

* * *

I know I already covered the concept of hell in this book, but I want to take some time here to discuss death and the afterlife in sacred texts. Death permeates the Christian Bible, and it seems that "sin" is always punished by it.

Well, what then about all the good people who die, including children who couldn't possibly be full of this so-called sin? It's no wonder that after all these centuries of negativity piling upon itself and gaining power, humankind has either been so scared about death or just wishes that it would all be over with. This malaise settles on us, and we become as our Lord says: spiritually poor. There's nothing to look back on, or forward to, because we supposedly even come into life full of sin. The tragedy is that many of us have bought all this hook, line, and sinker.

In addition, Christianity has made so much more of hell than the other religions have (or at least their acknowledgment of the devil seems to have taken front and center). Other religions believe in karma, cause and effect, and forms of retribution, but they don't seem to have the gruesome sword of eternal damnation always hanging over their heads. I'm not criticizing—after all, we in Novus Spritus *are* Gnostic Christians—but rather am simply pointing out a way that so many of us have been reigned by fear.

As for purgatory and limbo, this is probably the most confusing part of Christianity (not just Catholicism). Even if there aren't such places, they seem to have infiltrated the collective consciousness of humankind. Before we get into this, let me say that I'm not just picking on one particular religion. So many of the world's faiths have a similar concept as purgatory, and it can vary in interpretation from one sect to another.

Now then, as believed by Catholics, purgatory is a place of temporary punishment for those who die in God's grace, but aren't completely free from venial (minor) sins or haven't entirely paid for their sins. Gnostics believe that some souls get caught in between dimensions because they don't know that they're dead (they're what we think of as ghosts). If we stretch this, we could see this behavior comes from unfinished business or a type of derangement, possibly caused by the type of death the individuals incurred. I've personally seen a holding place where entities who, out of despair, committed suicide. They were waiting to be released back into life, but weren't being punished in any way. So I hope you see here that there's a big difference between what someone decides to do as a reaction to stress, pressure, depression, or mental illness . . . and an outside entity judging where that person is going to spend eternity.

While I can somewhat see the argument for purgatory, limbo, on the other hand, has always been a bone of contention with me. Limbo is considered to be the place where unbaptized souls go, never to get out and see God. If that's true, then limbo is more full of souls than hell is. Think of all the people prior to the advent of Christianity (or even after) who didn't know about baptism.

Gnostics believe that we use baptism as a symbol to rinse away past-life negativities, and it's an optional sacrament. We certainly don't agree that an all-loving God would blame and condemn someone who not only wasn't baptized, but didn't even know He/She existed. What if they belonged to another religion that didn't believe in God? And what about a helpless baby who dies and doesn't get a chance to be baptized—how can that be loving or even rational?

At least the belief in purgatory and limbo isn't as dire as the Calvinistic notion that whether or not a person goes to heaven or hell is already set into stone before they're even born. Other sects such as the Jehovah's Witnesses believe that there will only be a certain number of souls who gain salvation—so even if everyone is good, some folks might not be saved. Then you have those who are certain that you have to believe in and be saved by Jesus Christ to reach heaven (and God pity those who have never heard of him). All of these notions are just ridiculous!

I also don't believe that God needs us to sit on a mountaintop meditating our life away, mutilate our bodies for religious purposes, or perform human sacrifice and murder in the name of what's "holy." This isn't a criticism, but rather a logical intellectual commentary on an all-knowing, all-loving, forgiving, and already-accepting God. I don't need to walk on coals of fire to prove I love Him/Her.

We put human-made dogma before God. God just wants us to live our lives as fully and happily as possible and then simply go Home. He/She doesn't want us to fear where we're going, but to live, do good deeds, and come back after death to the Other Side—which was made for us to live happily in for eternity.

It's so funny that we're afraid to live *and* afraid to die, and that only dogma is supposed to sustain us, when none of this ever came from the mouth of Christ. I had a priest tell me many years ago at a funeral that everyone who wanted to go to heaven got there. What a beautiful, simple concept. . . .

How Can This Tenet Help You?

When the time comes, you don't need to allow artificial means or machines to prolong your life—unless, of course, you choose them to. That doesn't mean that you shouldn't get medical or holistic aid, but you may reach the point when enough is enough. So if the cure becomes worse than the illness, you have the right to say, "Let God's will be done."

You also have every right to preserve life—and it's never okay for you to cause anyone else's death with assisted suicide, like Dr. Jack Kevorkian has done. At the same time, you have the right to remove life support when someone you care about has no chance to recover, would be a vegetable, or would simply be a body without mind and soul kept alive by machines. In these cases, the soul has already departed. I've never seen anyone hang around in a body that has no hope of recovery.

If you're faced with the decision of either keeping life support going or removing it for a loved one, you have my sympathies, because it's not an easy decision (especially if continuing it is financially draining). The first thing you must do is ascertain whether the patient has a chance for recovery. If they do, what quality of life will they have? If they're going to be in a coma forever or live without the benefit of their mind, then I can assure you that they're not there—and they would not want to be kept alive artificially.

Common sense dictates that if a person doesn't have a chance of recovery or living some type of quality existence with artificial support, then it should be removed and God will take it from there. To preserve a life because a machine can keep the heart beating and the lungs breathing isn't always fair to the patient or to the family, especially when the soul has already departed and is looking at the situation from the Other Side.

I remember when my 92-year-old mother was in a coma from pneumonia, and the doctor wanted to perform a thyroid test on her. I said, "Are you crazy?! She's dying."

His reply was, "Well, that *is* a problem," and left the room.

I told everyone to just allow Mother to be comfortable and to let her go. She went within the hour.

Similarly, when Grandma Ada was dying (also of pneumonia), I kept saying, "Grandma, I love you," even though she was unconscious. All of a sudden her pupils, which had been fixed, turned toward me in a moment of love and recognition—and we telepathically said our good-byes. I know in my bones that both my mother and grandmother went the way they would have wanted—peacefully, and without a long, drawn-out struggle to go Home.

So, as hard as it is, know that you must live for today—but also never fear death, which is the ultimate reward for living. After all, death is a celebration of *life*.

✻ ✻ ✻ ✻ ✻ ✻

TENET XIX

We believe in a Mother God, Who is co-Creator with our all-loving Father God.

I covered a lot of information about this subject in my book *Mother God,* but there's still so much out there in terms of researching how the matriarchal principle has always raised her head throughout history.

The fact is, pure logic dictates that if there is a male principle, there has to be a female counterpart. So in this tenet I'd like to briefly address this female deity (which we call Azna), and not just from an intellectual and emotional level. Who is She; what purpose does She play; and why do we pray to, petition, and—above all—love Her?

She's been called Theodora, Sophia, Isis, Hera, the Mother Goddess, and a hundred other names by ancient humankind, as well as by many religions. My guide Francine says that Her visage can change to make Her more relatable to all people: She can be African, Asian, Arabian, Latino, Polynesian, or representative of any culture—which, of course, shows that She is all things to all people.

Darren English, one of Novus Spiritus's cardinals and a great researcher, has tracked so much of the Gnostic movement around the world, from Qumran (near the Dead Sea) to France. The information he's discovered (with the aid of Francine's direction) has been truly amazing, and I use much of it in my books where pertinent. Notwithstanding the fact that he's been a great addition to our movement, Darren has also been with me on many trips, particularly to Egypt, France, Greece, and Turkey, where we viewed and explored various temples of the Goddess.

In our travels, Darren and I have had many interactions with the local populace of each country, and we've found that a great number of them believe in the Mother God or Goddess. They generally keep quiet about it, as many of them belong to a religion that doesn't condone the belief in Her, but they believe inwardly. It's strange how it manifested when Darren and I started talking about the Mother God with these people: When they heard our views, they came out in the open and fervently praised Her and extolled Her virtues, especially in answering their prayers to Her.

For years I've noticed that She is alive and well all over the globe. In fact, I was talking to a client in Japan recently who has some of my translated books. She said, "We have always believed in a female deity, the yin and yang so to speak, and we cannot understand why this concept would be so hard for your country to accept."

The only place in America that really seems to get Azna is Hawaii, where she's referred to as Pele. Native Hawaiians still believe in their ancient religious practices, with *kahunas* (shaman priests) handing down to this day their ancient teachings, which are wonderful and deal so much with nature and its forces. They believe that they're protected by the devas of nature, with Pele controlling volcanoes. Of course, Hawaiians have a long and storied history with gods and goddesses, myths and legends, and heroes and mystical beings, such as the Menehunes, or the little people of Hawaii.

Regardless of the various visages that She takes, when She's seen on the Other Side (which is quite frequently), She tends to be garbed in a golden breastplate; a short, Roman-style tunic and skirt; and golden arm guards—although at times she'll appear in flowing, beautiful dresses, especially if She's in the Rose Garden. She has a voluptuous, Rubenesque type of figure and long, burnished-red hair; and she's tall, with a beautiful face and smile.

Azna always carries a golden sword, which is just a symbol of Her fighting darkness and cutting through evil. We Gnostics use it as a symbol (alongside the three trinity circles of loyalty, gratitude, and commitment) because the sword also makes a cross. I've always believed that you use or make available any symbol that carries positive energy with it, and the cross is certainly that.

Just like Father God, Mother God has always been a Creator. Some believe that She was the *primary* Creator, but that would make our Father fallible and less than She. No, they've both always been in existence, just as all of us have. However, She *is* visually accessible, while He usually chooses not to hold a form for very long, even on the Other Side. She's the activator, the grand interceptor of negativity, and She even has the ability to change charts. She rules over this planet, which makes Her more available to us. Does that make Her more powerful? No, it's just the definite delineation of power.

Azna is like the Heart of this planetary school, while Father God is the Head. We all emulate our Divine Parents: We're emotional *and* intellectual, with the emotional side being Mother God, and the intellectual side being Father God.

Now for eons ancient cultures worshiped the Mother God or Goddess. Religions that practiced polytheism are now considered to be pagan, but the civilizations that did so, such as those in Rome, Greece, Persia, and Egypt, ruled the world for centuries. They brought us art, music, writing, and fundamental truths and laws that still exist today. If you've researched and studied these ancient religions, then you know as I do the beauty and simplicity of their beliefs, which have been submerged and suppressed by the power and wealth of today's modern religions.

In more recent times, Mother God has appeared to look like the pictures we've seen of Mary the Blessed Virgin—which is how she appeared to the children of Fatima, to St. Bernadette at Lourdes, or to the people of Guadalupe. Francine says that She appears like this so that She will be seen in the dress of Christ's time. Yet with the advent of Christianity, Azna was suppressed and almost totally erased. The way they got around the issue was to give us Mary, the mother of Christ, as a substitution for the Mother God, Who is truly our co-Creator.

Although the Christian movement has taken great pains to hide the truth for so many years, little bits and pieces are coming out these days, and the media is taking notice and picking up on the feminine principle. Books such as the aforementioned *Holy Blood, Holy Grail; The Messianic Legacy;* and *The Da Vinci Code* have brought some of these truths out of the proverbial closet and into the public eye. I realize that much of this information addresses Mary and Mary Magdalene, but no one seems to be brave enough to boldly come out and scream, "All right, you have the tail of the elephant—now get the whole thing!"

No one is to blame for this—after all, it's easier for a salmon to swim upstream than it is for us to fly in the face of patriarchal religions. They have their mean and fearful male God and don't want the applecart upset with a loving God, especially if it's a loving *Mother* God. I don't understand why faith has to come into play when logic and plain ol' deductive reasoning show the way.

They used to say when I was in Catholic school that "if God closes the door, Mary will open the window." I'm sure they didn't know how close they were to the ultimate truth. Let's face it, in the early days of the Gnostic Christians (which our Lord was), women were oftentimes the ministers. They'd perform a type of holy religious service, but would also do healings and tell stories of Jesus. When their popularity began to grow, the early apostolic movement decided that this wouldn't work because the Bible says that women are second-class citizens. Apparently they felt that it would go against their own religion—especially the outdated writings of the Old Testament—to elevate women.

Please keep in mind that the Bible wasn't even fully compiled until around A.D. 300, and if it hadn't been for Constantine and his making it the official religion of the Roman empire, I'm sure that Christianity would have gone by the wayside. Its popularity was dwindling because of the Roman persecutions and the splintering off of different sects that often had to meet secretly or be killed. And it had begun to falter because there was no leader and no cohesive organization.

The minute Constantine took over, however, he put in place only the parts of the Bible *he* wanted, and established Christianity to be the patriarchal state religion of the Roman empire . . . and then he declared himself the religion's hero for saving it from extinction. Yet, ironically, Francine says that when Christ was hanging on the cross and said, "Father, forgive them, for they know not what they do," he was speaking to Father God. However, when he said, "Mother, behold thy son," even though everyone assumes that he was talking to his earthly mother, Mary, he was in fact addressing his Mother in heaven.

It seems that the pendulum had to swing to one side (patriarchal religion), and now it's beginning to come back. But please understand that I don't want to see a matriarchal religion—I'd rather that we embrace one that recognizes *both* the Mother and Father from which we all were created.

There are now archaeological theories stating that some of Crete, Egypt, and the Greek Isles was actually part of Atlantis, the long-lost continent located in the Atlantic Ocean that sank many thousands of years ago. There are a number of caves in these regions that have pictographs that show what looks like a female deity or being of power. Francine says that in Atlantis and Lemuria (the lost continent in the Pacific Ocean), the female Goddess was alive and well. Now keep in mind that this would have been thousands of years before Christ was born.

It's interesting to note that we at Novus Spiritus have always been devoted to the Mother God, long before we ever revealed this to the general public through my books. People who came in for regressions would more times than not immediately see the Other Side when taken to a death in a past life. They'd invariably see themselves in the Hall of Wisdom, Hall of Justice, or Hall of Records—places where they viewed their just-lived lives, went over their charts, or met with all their loved ones.

Many of these same people would also see a statue of a beautiful woman dressed in golden armor with a sword at her side. When asked who she was, without hesitation and regardless of what religious beliefs they came from, they'd almost always say, "The Mother God, of course." The replies were so matter-of-fact that it was almost as if we were stupid that we didn't know, or even asked the question at all.

* * *

You know, whether you see me as controversial or not, I'm now at the age where I just try to put forth the truth, and so it is with the Mother God. Whether you believe in Her or not—or if you call Her Sophia, Mary, Theodora, or the Anatole—She is the one in the duality of Creators who performs miracles and eliminates negativity. So if you pray to Her, She will answer.

The stories that have come out of the e-mails my office receives, along with the readings that my son and I do, are numerous and legendary. Not a day goes by that we don't hear of a petition being answered or a miracle being performed by Azna. Most of the missives have the common denominator of being the last hope for help—they often concern near-death concerns, life-threatening illness, calamities of every nature, legal cases, and so on. And in almost every case, whenever our ministers have petitioned Mother God for help or a miracle, the person is healed, custody of a child is won in court, a divorce is reversed, cancer is cured, and on and on it goes. In other words, miracle after miracle occurs.

I personally have no problem petitioning her for any- and everything, from "Please, Mother, don't let the plane be delayed" to the larger problems of my last divorce, which could have been ugly but wasn't (well . . . at least I'll say that it could have been so much more horrific than it was). I petition to protect my loved ones, people I read for, and the planet; my personal health and finances; and so much more. In almost every case, we seem to get right down to the wire, but she always comes through.

I never fail to be amused when I hear someone ask, "Aren't you afraid that you're bothering Her or asking for too much?" No, because we can't . . . for then we'd be putting Her in the same category that we've put Father God into—that is, we make Them aggravated and humanistic like we are. Once and for all, They can't be—*They're perfect, all-loving Beings.*

The only time we human beings get into trouble is when we go into that vanity mode of entitlement—we need something above everything else, or we want something that will hurt another person. In these types of situations, we're not going to get our prayers answered. But trust me, if we're under Her mantle of protection and live a good life, She'll mete out justice.

I always ask Her for protection for myself and others, whether it's verbally or even in writing: I write Her letters or notes and then burn them to request Her help before I do my readings, for example. I encourage people to not only petition Her, but Her army of the phylum of angels called the Thrones as well. This is Her army, the same as the phylum of angels called Principalities are Father God's army.

Every night I petition Her and Her Thrones. But of course, I also call on God the Father and His Principalities, our Lord, and the Holy Spirit (which is really just the love between Mother and Father God that sends grace, strength, protection, and prosperity) to protect my family and loved ones. In addition, I petition Azna for the animals and things that pertain to earthly life.

My devotion to Her has been unwavering. Just to give you what might seem like a mundane example of how I rely on Her help, I had to get to Los Angeles for some important business. At the time there were horrible storms raging in both the San Jose area (about 50 miles south of San Francisco) and in Southern California that included high winds and torrential rains. My assistant, Michael, and I had to go by plane because the highways were closed, but all aircraft was delayed or grounded.

I said, "Please, Mother, get us out." Michael and I went to the airport knowing already that our original flight was delayed a minimum of three hours. As we got to check-in, we found that our flight was indeed pushed back for at least four hours, but the airline had an earlier flight to the same destination. We jumped at the chance to take it, and it left at almost the same time as our original flight had been scheduled to take off. We found out later that right after we took off, all subsequent flights had been grounded and didn't leave until the next day. Now you can say, "Well, Sylvia, that's just coincidence or luck." Yes, I guess you could say that . . . until you try it for yourself.

I'm also reminded of when I was in Houston and got a call that my granddaughter had her lip bitten by a dog. I couldn't get out, so I prayed to Mother God all night. When I got home, I was told that it was a miracle: Angelia's lip, which should have been torn off, was split but inverted on itself, so they pulled it forward and stitched it. She's since had two surgeries to correct it, but the miracle is that when they first looked at it, the lip appeared to be missing. A mistake from two specialists? I think not. . . .

These are just a few of my stories—I could go on and on. The letters my office has received about Mother God are all categorized in our research files, and you start to notice when certain things keep happening. There can't be *that* many coincidences in the world. As I've said, what does it hurt to give it a try? Call Her Mary, Azna, or whatever; but She (like our Lord or Father God) will answer to any call— the point is, just call.

How Can This Tenet Help You?

As I often say, you don't have to believe in any of this— or just take with you what you want—but for the sake of even skepticism, you should just try calling on Mother God. All of my study groups and ministers, who now range in the thousands, pray to Her, and it seems that not a day goes by that I don't hear of a miracle when She's called upon. She's also the spiritual leader of the prayer line that's dedicated to Her—and the results of that line border on the fantastic. (For more information about our prayer line, please visit **www. sylvia.org.**)

If you decide to pray to Azna for help, you can ask Her for your children's sake, your pets, or yourself—even what may seem like petty concerns are never that in Her eyes. By asking, you'll just reinforce the bond you have with Her, and will open the once-closed door for Her to enter your life and show you beyond any doubt what real creative power is. You needn't worry if your prayers are being answered or not.

Of course not *everything* is going to be granted, and praying to Her is not a fix-all or magic bullet. After all, She won't change your chart so drastically that you won't learn, and you're not always going to get your way. But things will get modified, miracles will happen, and things that are negative will turn around faster for the better. She also doles out karma in the sense that She rights wrongs very swiftly.

Ask for proof through your petitions. I don't have any fear that you'll fail to be surprised or convinced (if you're not already). And never forget about our Father, Jesus, the angels, and our guides—if anything, there's so much help available that we don't even utilize it!

* * * * * *

TENET XX

*We believe that our Lord was crucified,
but did not die on the cross. Instead, he went
on to live his life in France with his mother
and Mary Magdalene, his wife.*

Dan Brown's book *The Da Vinci Code* has really piqued the public's interest. Although it's a fictional work that has stayed on the bestseller list for more than two years, the book is actually filled with factual research about secrets that have been kept for years. All the controversy and curiosity it's provoked will only make researchers delve more into these secrets and come out with the truths that have been suppressed and hidden for centuries.

I personally loved this book, and although some facts may have been embellished a bit, the basic information is entirely true. In fact, we at Novus Spiritus have believed this for many years, and I even covered the subject of Jesus' "death" and lost years in detail in my book *Secrets & Mysteries of the World*. However, in the event that you haven't read either of the above-mentioned books, I'd like to take this opportunity to introduce you to the mystery and phenomenon that is Mary Magdalene, since she was an integral part of Christ's life.

As there are groups and organizations that believe that Jesus Christ was a myth, so are there many who say that the Crucifixion never took place. In my research, I've found that the Crucifixion *did* happen . . . but then I part ways with what many Christians believe (specifically, that Jesus died on the cross).

You see, the scriptures tell us that Pontius Pilate didn't want to crucify Christ. He was even told by his wife that she'd had a dream it would be wrong. He wanted to wash his hands of it, which he literally did, and sent Jesus back from his initial audience, saying that he could find no wrong in what the young prophet had done. Christ was condemned mainly because he was a danger to the traditional Judaic religion, and the Romans didn't want any chance of an uprising to occur. He wasn't against anyone except hypocrites, and he only wanted to put forth the concept of an all-loving God—and for that, he was crucified.

My research, however, unearthed a very plausible plot to save his life. He had many friends, some of whom were fairly wealthy—it's been surmised that a few of them bribed Pontius Pilate in order to save the Messiah's life. Joseph of Arimathea is believed to be the head of this conspiracy; coincidentally, it was his tomb in which Jesus was laid. In fact, coincidence follows coincidence.

Consider the following facts:

1. It normally took several days for people to die on the cross, which was why the Romans preferred it as a form of execution. However, Pontius Pilate made sure that Christ only had to spend a few hours on the cross because he was crucified just before the Jewish Sabbath Day, on which no one could be crucified.

2. Crucifixion victims had their legs broken so that they couldn't lift themselves up to breathe. (Asphyxiation was the normal cause of death due to compression of the lungs while hanging.) Jesus' legs were never broken, which allowed him to rest his feet and lift himself up.

3. Christ was a healthy young male of 33 and would have had a lot of stamina.

4. He was taken down from the cross by friends who put him in an above-ground tomb, and he was never buried. Therefore, he would have been able to get out of the tomb.

Skeptics will point out, "But they pierced his side." Well, Francine says that this was actually a symbolic scratch—the vinegar and gaul acted as an anesthetic that ended Jesus' pain and rendered him unconscious in an *assimilated* death. It's like if you were under anesthesia, you might appear limp and dead to the uneducated or nonmedical mind.

We have other evidence that relates to Christ's survival, and ironically it comes from scripture. In Luke 24:5, the angels in the tomb said to Mary and Mary Magdalene, "Why do you look for the living among the dead?" Later, Jesus appeared to his apostles to prove that he was still alive, but they were startled and panic-stricken, thinking that they saw a spirit. "And he said to them, 'Why are you disturbed, and why do doubts arise in your hearts? See my hands and feet, that it is I myself. Feel me and see; for a spirit does not have flesh and bones, as you see I have.' And having said this, he showed them his hands and his feet. But as they still disbelieved and marveled for joy, he said, 'Have you anything here to eat?' And they offered him a piece of broiled fish and a honeycomb. And when he had eaten in their presence, he took what remained and gave it to them."

Even when Mary Magdalene tried to tell the other

apostles that Christ was alive, they didn't believe her. Not until he showed up at the room where they were hiding did they understand that he wasn't a ghost. Jesus even has Thomas put his hands into his wounds to show he still lived (thus the expression "doubting Thomas"). Now I've had a lot of experience with ghosts, and believe me, they don't eat, you can't feel the solidity of their bodies, and they definitely don't carry healing wounds. These incidents can only be explained by the fact that Jesus had survived the Crucifixion.

Christ fulfilled his chart by going through the trial, scourging, humiliation of carrying his own cross, and of course the Crucifixion—the fact that he didn't die on the cross doesn't take away his divinity or his teachings. In fact, his teachings were so important that he continued them in other parts of the world.

Our Lord was not stupid, and he knew that he had to get away from Jerusalem or risk being caught again. So he left his disciples with instructions and went off with his mother and Mary Magdalene to greener pastures. It's amazing to believe that in his lifetime he was certainly loved, but he was also ridiculed, ostracized, and even called "the evil prince [or king]." It seems that the idea of love just doesn't take too well in this world. It seems to fly in the face of those who would rather have a fearful, vengeful, and humanized God. Of course this concept also has a tendency to keep people in line and thereby under control.

* * *

The following is from an article that Darren English wrote for our Novus Spiritus newsletter. I think it's really amazing, and even though it's somewhat long, it adds a lot to the issues of this section.

How Do You Know What You Know?
(From *Novus Connection,* January 2005)

We make judgments based on our personal experiences that color our makeup as a person. Sylvia tells us we can judge the action, but not the soul, of the person. We must be careful of making judgments, even if we are just judging the action, because not far from judging the action comes ascribing a motive, which is quickly followed by making a judgment of the soul.

We learn through experience, research, listening, discernment, and infusion; but tradition [also] plays a large part in our learning. As anyone in the office will tell you, I love reading. I especially enjoy reading history, including the history of Gnosticism. However, we can't look at history and suppose we can understand the motivation of the characters involved. . . .

What do we know or think we know about Mary Magdalene? What did Mary Magdalene do for a living before she met Jesus? We've been told that she was a prostitute. It's in the Bible—right? Nowhere does it say in the Bible that Mary Magdalene was a harlot. So how did [she] get labeled a prostitute?

We need to remember that we can't judge history or historical figures from our 21st-century perspective. In A.D. 591, Pope Gregory I gave a sermon that included information about Mary [Magdalene]. In Luke 8, it says that Jesus cast out seven demons from Mary Magdalene. Pope Gregory said that the seven demons represented the seven deadly sins. He also stated that Mary Magdalene was the woman identified in Luke as the woman living a life of sin, who anointed Jesus' feet with perfumed oils. Pope Gregory stated that she used these perfumes in her profession as a prostitute. From 591 on, Mary Magdalene was labeled a harlot. Did you know that in 1969 the Catholic Church repealed the declaration that Mary Magdalene was a prostitute? Unfortunately, once an accusation has been made

[or] once someone has been labeled, even falsely, the stain of that accusation lingers on. . . .

So the traditional teaching of Mary Magdalene wasn't correct. It's easy to start pointing our little Gnostic fingers at Pope Gregory and say that he was motivated by misogyny, that he was trying to squelch the feminine principle by labeling Mary Magdalene a prostitute. I don't know what his motivation was, but the result of this mislabeling and misinformation was used as a powerful illustration of Christ's perfect love, of God's perfect love. The idea that Mary Magdalene was forgiven and embraced by Jesus became a beautiful example of the love that God holds for each of us—no matter how we regard ourselves, no matter how low an opinion others have of us, God is still there, loving us all as His children. Mary became St. Mary Magdalene, the Saint of Repentance; her feast day is July 22.

So who is this woman, Mary Magdalene, if she wasn't the repentant prostitute that we've known her as for so many years? The name *Magdalene* may have denoted her hometown of Magdala on the shore of Galilee, or it may have been a title. In Aramaic, *Magdala* means "Tower." So Mary the Magdalene may have been a title, similar to "Mary the Great," or "Mary of Towering Faith."

In the Gospels, [she] is portrayed as not a primary disciple, but as one of the women who traveled with Jesus and his disciples and supported them monetarily in their ministry. Mary Magdalene, however, was one of the few of Jesus' followers present at the Crucifixion, not his mother, Mary. Most of the male disciples were in hiding, afraid that they might be arrested and crucified [also]. Mary Magdalene was the first to visit the tomb where Christ was placed and witnessed the risen Christ. She is actually known as the "Apostle to the Apostles," because it was she who brought the news to the disciples that Jesus was not dead.

We know Mary not only from the New Testament Gospels but also from the Gnostic Gospels of Mary Magdalene, the Gospel of Phillip, the Gospel of Thomas, the Pistis Sophia, and the Dialogue of the Savior run in. These texts give us a different picture of Mary Magdalene than we see in the New Testament Gospels. Through the[m], we find that she was not only a follower of Jesus, but [his] confidant and closest spiritual companion, his consort, and a primary apostolic figure in the early Christian church. According to the Gospel of Phillip, Mary is the one who Jesus loved the most and "kissed often on the mouth."

In [a] 1979 trance, Francine said that "Christ had a very beautiful love affair with Mary Magdalene, actually like a soul-mate concept. They were very deeply in love with each other." In the Gospel of Mary Magdalene, Peter says, "We know the savior loved you more than any other woman." Peter then asks Mary to tell him and the other disciples what teachings Jesus shared with her in private. . . .

Raheim, a second guide of Sylvia's who also speaks through Sylvia during trance, tells us that when Mary Magdalene anointed Jesus' feet with perfumed oils, it was an anointment of ritual, [but] she was actually [also] using a form of therapeutic massage or reflexology to tend to him. We read over and over in the Bible that Jesus healed and tended to the sick, but Mary Magdalene and Mary, his mother, are the only figures in the Bible to tend to Jesus.

The verse in Luke where we read that Jesus cast out seven demons from Mary Magdalene still bothered me a bit, until I started to think about it from a wider perspective. In the ancient world any illness was seen as being caused not by a virus, but by a demon. During his formative years prior to beginning his ministry, Jesus studied not only Jewish/Hebrew texts, but also studied in India and Tibet and would have certainly have known of chakras and energy healing. I asked Sylvia if this "casting out of demons" wasn't actually a chakra cleansing. [She] said yes, it was a chakra cleansing as opposed to an exorcism that Jesus performed on Mary.

Francine tells us that Jesus was "trying to bring the

female principle forward, whether it was Mary Magdalene or his mother." Gnostic tradition tells us that Mary Magdalene was a principal figure in the early church. By reading the Gnostic Gospels in conjunction with the New Testament Gospels, we get a much wider picture of Mary Magdalene and her teachings as a woman who was able to "turn the disciple's hearts to the good" to the Christ Consciousness within. . . .

So ask yourself, how do you know what you know? Are you holding on to illusions that you've adopted as tradition? Question everything you think you know. But know this: No matter what anyone says about you, no matter what they think of you, our God the Mother and God the Father love you very much, and nothing you do [or] say will ever change that.

For generations the Cathars and the Knights Templar have known all this information, and they fought to the death to keep the secret of Christ's continued life. Yet it's awfully hard for the Catholic Church to accept the fact that Jesus married Mary Magdalene, especially after they'd worked the scripture to make her look like a harlot.

It's strange, though—over the years Mary has not only been canonized, but in France there's the church of "The Magdalene." Why would the Church retract what they've said? Well, there could be a very simple explanation: They know the truth. Maybe they're just covering their tracks, especially when you consider that the Vatican contains thousands of writings that are kept in vaults that no one can see. It would be hard to imagine that the Church doesn't know the truth, especially when they had the wealth and power to get it if they so chose. Certainly the same truth that's been researched lately would have been available to their scholars and researchers.

All of this is a delicate matter for the Church—after all, how do they handle this truth when it goes against what they've been teaching for the last 2,000 years? It would certainly rock their foundations and create utter chaos among the faithful . . . which is probably why they'll never overtly let the truth out. However, we *have* gotten little tidbits of what they know, such as when Pope John XXIII said, "Christ's Crucifixion or his death or life should not affect our belief."

Maybe as time goes by, the Church will try to ease the faithful into the truth—unless, of course, it blows up in their face. And let's be honest here: The Catholic Church is a powerful organization, and past practice has seen them move exceedingly slow in acknowledging their mistakes. Nevertheless, truth is truth, and whether or not you believe that Jesus lived or died after his crucifixion shouldn't affect Christianity—I've always believed that the *teachings* of Christ are the real cornerstones of Christianity, not whether he died on a cross and was subsequently resurrected. After all, each and every one of us resurrects when we die.

How Can This Tenet Help You?

Before you read on, I'd like you to think about *The Last Supper* by Leonardo da Vinci. (In fact, if you can, please look at the painting for a minute.) Now I defy anyone not to notice that the person sitting to Christ's right is a female, who I believe is Mary Magdalene. Yet for so many years my eyes went directly to our Lord rather than to the other apostles—no matter how many times I looked at and contemplated the meaning of this work of art, I never noticed this female until it was pointed out in *The Da Vinci Code*.

This book has given those of us who've read it pause for thought, and in many cases, a different perspective. It's a known fact that the mind sees what it's been programmed to see, and we bring our own beliefs and agendas with us—so we often miss the things that are right in front of us. I want you to keep that in mind as you ponder this tenet.

Mary Magdalene was the most devoted of any of the apostles (in fact, some theologians have taken to calling her the first real apostle). She washed Jesus' feet, traveled with him, and was by his side during the Crucifixion and afterward. They loved each other and left together after his mission was complete.

If you think it's terrible to even speculate that a true messiah and messenger had a life with a woman who loved him, research it for yourself. Read and peruse the Bible, the Gnostic texts, and the Gnostic Gospels that were found at Nag Hammadi, and you'll find Christ's love for Mary Magdalene. Now if *this* has been swept under the rug, what makes you think that the fear of the feminine principle (which our Lord tried so hard to elevate), wouldn't also be hidden by the patriarchal rule?

If you look at the scriptures closely, Jesus didn't really fulfill what the Judaic religion had prophesied—that he was supposed to come as a king and free the Jews, as Moses did. What they didn't understand or see was that, as he said so often, "My kingdom is not of this world." In other words, he wanted people to know a loving God, not to take this life so seriously, and to look forward to going Home (to the Other Side). Since he was never accepted as their savior, Judaism is still waiting for their prophesied savior to appear.

Christ was truly an Essene and a Gnostic. While the scriptures say that he ascended into heaven, it's interesting to note that the Essene community at Qumran (which was the center of Gnosticism) was called "heaven." Could this have meant that he just went to Qumran? Regardless, since Jesus was a messenger from God, it's not unlikely that he visited heaven and then came back again.

What this boils down to is that we *all* ascend into heaven, both at our death and throughout our lives by means of astral travel—most of us just aren't aware of it. So remember to keep your mind—and your heart—open.

* * * * * *

TENET XXI

*We Gnostics kept the knowledge hidden
that Christ's lineage exists even today,
and the truth long buried is open to research.*

In Dan Brown's book *Angels & Demons,* he writes about a group called "the Illuminati." Although this book is a work of fiction, Brown says that the brotherhood of the Illuminati is not. My spirit guide Francine says that it does indeed exist, as do many other "underground" organizations that have information about Christ's lineage.

Francine says that after Jesus fulfilled his commitment and left his apostles, he took the two Marys (his mother and Magdalene) and went from Jerusalem to Qumran. From there they traveled to Turkey and Kashmir, and finally ended up in France. When I was in Ankara, Turkey, I heard the local oral tradition stating that Christ, Mary, and Mary Magdalene visited there after his supposed death. The strange thing is that the Turks wouldn't have anything to gain, or lose for that matter, by giving out this information. . . .

It was in France that Jesus and Mary Magdalene (whom

he'd married) started a family. Francine goes on to say that they had three children, two boys and a girl; and that our Lord lived to be very old. However, he died before his wife, who spent the rest of her life in his ministry. (Is it a coincidence that in France they have the Church of the Magdalene and honor her as a saint?) Francine also says that she did a lot of writing after Jesus died, but these writings have yet to be found or are hidden and not for public view.

It's interesting to note that one of the largest Gnostic communities was in France. In fact, when I was in southern France one time, I was sitting on a rock, and a vision as clear as a bell came to me. Now I'm not often inclined to have real-life visions, like the ones they depict on TV or in the movies, but this one was incredible. In terms of clarity, it was similar to the one I had when I was at Stonehenge (which I related in my book *Secrets & Mysteries of the World*)—these are the two most vivid visions I've had.

When I see a past murder or crime, I can feel and view it, and I even get names and places, but these two visions were different: It's like I was going back in the records of time and viewing what went on as a third person—and it was so incredibly clear. I believe that we all undergo something similar when we experience déjà vu or a familiarity and longing for certain places, but this is like watching a movie . . . except you're part of it, and the smells and sounds are all around you. It's like a type of conscious trance.

Anyway, what I saw in France began with myself and others winding our way through a forest near dusk. It felt like spring because flowers were beginning to bloom, and we seemed to be on our way toward Montsegur in the Languedoc region, where the Gnostics had a community. Many of those around me were dressed in coarse brown robes, almost like the Franciscans wore, with ropes around their waists. The women's long hair was covered by plain muslin scarves; while the men had their heads shaved, again like the early monks with a tonsure. We all had on rough-hewn sandals with rope straps—I noticed this because my right ankle hurt from the rub of the rope. Some were carrying baskets of fruit, some were carrying grain, and some were pulling goats; while the young ones helped out the elderly—but we all were singing softly.

I'm fairly fluent in French, so I could make out the words *mon dieu* ("my God") as we finally arrived at this type of castle, which didn't seem at all unfamiliar. Other people had already arrived, and seemed to be pulled toward this beautiful man who was standing there with a very attractive dark-haired woman. There was an older lady sitting on a rock, and children were playing nearby. I knew that we were in the presence of the Holy Family, and our allegiance was unquestionable.

We all sat down and listened to what lies beyond this life: the Other Side and the lessons we're all here to learn. It seemed, in fact, as if the whole Gnostic philosophy was unfolding before me. The group I was with then ate and drank, and we returned to our village much later. It seemed that we'd given homage to the Mother God and were now coming back to finish the circle by honoring our Lord—and that we'd made this pilgrimage many times. I remember our Lord saying that it would be many years before the truth would come to the consciousness of humankind. And with that, my vision ended . . . but I will keep it with me for the rest of my life.

No matter if you believe my vision—or this subject—it's absolutely true that information about Christ's survival and his lineage has long been buried and hidden by the Cathars, Knights Templar, and other Gnostic groups that existed in the Middle Ages.

The Cathars were one of the early Gnostic sects of Christianity that believed that the soul goes from body to body until it reaches perfection. Essential acts in their rituals included a kiss on both sides of the cheeks (is this where the typical French greeting came from?) and a blowing on the hands (giving the breath of life and healing and the ability to heal). As such, they were often called the "good men" in their travels. The Cathars were very simplistic and journeyed together, preaching and talking to the people in fields, farmhouses, or barns; and they accepted women gladly into their communities.

While the Cathars seemed to be the teachers, the Knights Templar were the protectors. Formed during the Crusades to protect pilgrims on their way to Jerusalem, the Knights Templar later became the protectors of the secret about Christ's survival and lineage.

The proof that the Cathars and Knights Templar hid is guarded today by such modern-day organizations as the Illuminati, Masons, Rosicrucians, and Priory of Sion. It's also been suggested that these groups hold such treasures as the Ark of the Covenant and the Holy Grail, and they know where Christ's body is buried (among other things). They've kept this knowledge for centuries, building mystery upon mystery behind secret codes, meanings, rituals, and puzzles as a means of shrouding and protecting their knowledge and treasures; and to shield themselves from what they feel is the politically run machine of Christianity.

What is the agenda of these groups? Do they want to bring to power the lineage of Christ, which has been surmised in *Holy Blood, Holy Grail,* or do they have something entirely different planned? In time, I believe that we'll all find out, as researchers by the dozens are investigating these mysteries . . . but in the meantime, little bits and pieces of truth will be let out systematically so as not to unduly shock anyone.

You might wonder why (supposing these underground organizations do exist) they don't just come out with their knowledge. Since I don't belong to any of them, I can't presume to know the answer and can only ask the question. Oh, we can speculate that these groups went underground for fear of persecution, but would that apply today? Having lived for almost 70 years, I can give you my opinion: You bet it would!

Can you imagine the repercussions, which in all likelihood

would be global in proportion? Why invite a glut of media and attacks by Christians all over the world, leave yourself open to ridicule, be accused of being anti-Christ (or of being *the* anti-Christ), make enemies in the millions, and lose the anonymity of your group? It's for these reasons that I believe these organizations from time to time "leak" material or information in the form of new discoveries.

The authors of the books that have stirred up such controversy in recent years discovered so much enlightening information that other seekers have flocked to their sources (including France's Bibliothèque Nationale, which had to limit access to research because of so many requests). These writers have found bits and pieces of information that when put together certainly make a strong case for Christ's having offspring——and that his lineage continues to this day.

* * *

Since we've gone through the tenets that set the cornerstones for the Gnostic Christian beliefs of Novus Spiritus, I now want to delve further into religion . . . not to criticize or discriminate against anyone, but to show you how we really don't differ that wildly except for our beliefs regarding the Crucifixion and Mother God. But if you research as I have (and I hope you do), you'll see that the truths become overwhelming. Gnostic belief has historically been the *true* Christianity. It's simpler than some of the dogma we've been exposed to, but hopefully like me you'll hear our blessed Lord's words and think of him smiling as he said them. The reason I say this is because it's a shame that all we seem to remember is Christ in his agony on a cross—not the laughing Christ, the healing Christ, the God-loving Christ, Christ the man, Christ the friend, Christ the messenger, and Christ the teacher of the love of a perfect God.

I believe with all my heart that Jesus himself had a hand in the Gnostic Gospels because they were found at Nag Hammadi untarnished by humans. Yes, some previously known works were found—which shows that even then, there was a pecking order as far as what should be kept and what should be destroyed. The manuscripts appear to have been hidden because of a religious purge or a hunt for heretics and heretical material by the mainline Christian church, so they weren't edited, thanks to the morality or control for the day. As **www.religioustolerance.org** states:

> In 1945, Mohammed Ali es Samman, a Muslim camel driver from El Qasr in Egypt, went with his brother to a cliff near Nag Hammadi, a village in northern Egypt. They were digging for nitrate-rich earth that they could use for fertilizer. They came across a large clay jar buried in the ground. They were undecided whether to open it. They feared that it might contain an evil spirit; but they also suspected that it might contain gold or other material of great value. It turns out that their second guess was closer to the truth: the jar contained a library of Gnostic material of immeasurable value. Thirteen volumes survive, comprising 51 different works on 1153 pages. Six were copies of works already known; six others were duplicated within the library, and 41 were new, previously unknown works. Included were the *Gospel of Thomas, Gospel of Truth, Treatise on the Resurrection, Gospel of Phillip, Wisdom of Jesus Christ, Revelation of James, Letter of Peter to Phillip, On the Origin of the World,* and other writings. Of these, the Gospel of Thomas is considered the most important. It was a collection of the sayings of Jesus which were recorded very early in the Christian era. A later Gnostic author edited the Gospel. Some liberal theologians rank it equal in importance to the four Gospels of the Christian Scriptures.

In his book *The Gnostics,* Jaques Lacarriere defines Gnosticism as follows: "[It] is in essence a genesis restoring to man his true birth and overcomes his genetic and mental impurity." Although, as stated earlier, there were many different beliefs in Gnosticism and many different schools of thought, almost all Gnostics have come together on some key points:

1. We believe that mainline Christianity misunderstood Christ's mission on Earth, and Gnostic practices truly understood his message of love. Therefore, Gnostic practitioners are the only ones actually doing and continuing Christ's ministry.

2. Gnostic devotion to the gaining of knowledge is not just intellectual in nature. We believe that knowledge is the key to salvation; consequently, we read countless texts from other religions, garner the bits of truth in each of them as our own, and practice them. We also believe that knowledge is gained from experience, and in doing so, the soul must utilize the truths gained for salvation. All Gnostics believe that knowledge of and for the soul is paramount.

3. We believe in the male and female principles of God—just as there is duality in nature, so is there in God. The Mother God is worshiped as well as the Father God.

4. We believe that the soul or spirit is Divinely good and that the body and the earth are filled with evil and temptation. We believe that there is a spark of God in all of us due to Mother God's putting in the seeds of life.

5. We believe that each of us can attain his or her own personal peace and harmony by realizing that we are a Divine spark of God. Death allows us to escape this earthly plane and ascend and be reunited with God (salvation).

6. We do not look upon the world as having been created perfectly because we need to perfect and gain knowledge for the soul.

Little has been written about how ancient Gnostic groups functioned, but Francine goes along with what some theologians and historians have supposed: For many years, Gnostics who didn't really have a place to practice were solitary practitioners. (You don't realize how many e-mails and letters I got when my *Journey of the Soul* books came out that said, "I always believed this way but felt I was all alone.") Others were probably members of mainline Christian congregations, but they formed their own cliques within each church.

Until recently, there was no consensus on a "canon of Gnostic scripture," although many books that have been circulated over the years prefaced their own rendition. Now, however, thanks to Elaine Pagels and Barbara Thiering and their writings and compilations of Gnostic texts, we have what we've been waiting for. So if you want to research as I have, then a good place to start are their works. In addition, there are so many books coming out that are not only exposing what the original truth was, but comparing it to what has become "truth" politically over time. Once the truth is out, then people can make their own decisions about their belief system in an educated and logical manner, without having to wade through the half-truths and lies that have been perpetuated over the centuries.

Gnostics have always insisted that ignorance, not sin, causes us the mental and physical suffering that then leads to the suffering of the soul. Much like our modern psychotherapy, without self-knowledge, humans are led by compulsions and impulses that we don't understand or know. The truth, whatever that means to you, will set your soul free—your love of an all-loving God will grow, and your soul will find peace in the simple truths.

Just as our Lord said, the one theme that keeps repeating in Gnosticism is: "The kingdom of God is inside of you." This is probably one of the most powerful of Christ's teachings, and he reiterates it in many times in many different ways. It tells us that we'll find such a kingdom not only in our intelligence, but in our emotions, and acts of good toward others.

I feel with this enlightened age of search and research that each of us has begun to embark upon our own journey for spirituality, and to find the true Christ Consciousness within our own heart and soul—after all, the words of Jesus were what the Gnostics lived by and still do.

How Can This Tenet Help You?

You'll find your truth if you keep your mind and soul open. You don't need me or anyone else to tell you that things are really simpler than we've made them over the last 2,000 years. And remember that it's not just Christianity that has split off radical and close-minded sects. The fundamentalists of any religion are strict to the point of being prejudicial, judgmental, and lacking in love and compassion. Of course they hide it under the excuse that they're following scripture to the letter, but it's their *interpretation* that's flawed.

Also, many of these individuals' radical actions go against that very same scripture—that's how we get suicide bombers who kill thousands of innocents, or monks who douse themselves with gasoline and burn to death. Church rules and dogma oftentimes directly contradict the original words of the prophets who brought forth simple messages of love, for God and one another.

Even with all the attempts by the world's religious organizations to keep us mired in hate and fear, this feeling and tradition of a loving God has nevertheless crept in. I know this firsthand: When I was in Turkey and Egypt and talked to all the people who came with me on the trips, so many of the local citizens nearby would gather and listen. At first this was a little disconcerting because I never wanted any Muslims to think I was against them. But when I was invited to come on their television shows and had articles on me written in their newspapers, it was just the opposite. People on the street would come up to me and tell me that Mohammed preached love, and they always made me feel very welcome.

Love is the universal language that keeps this world going; unfortunately, the dark side plays its part with greed, ego, hate, and discrimination. So, regardless of what religion you aspire to, always remember that we have a *loving and forgiving God.* If someone tells you that unless you listen to or join them, you won't be saved, run away as fast as you can—or you're going to get caught in the trap of religious control and authority. In addition, if you just take what you're told as gospel and don't research your so-called belief systems, then you're not following Christ's words.

Children used to learn spirituality at home—just as the Judaic faith still ensures that its teachings become a family affair in the celebration of holidays such as Passover and Hanukah. This is as it should be. Spirituality ought to be part and parcel of our everyday lives, no matter what we believe in. In teaching our children, we must at least make them aware of other faiths and, if possible, have enough background in them to answer the kids' inevitable questions. If you do your research, you can be well versed in the different religions and faiths of this world and make a better choice for yourself—and you can also be a veritable well of information for your children, who may have questions about God or religious philosophies.

I personally believe in allowing young people to choose their own belief system when they can discern for themselves (after all, Jesus was only 12 when he was at the Temple teaching, while his mother and father were searching for him). But I also realize that many churches stress bringing kids into their parents' religion. It can cause conflict, but faith is such a personal thing that it shouldn't be chosen by another, for this will just create greater problems in the long run.

Consider this: Jesus himself went to the church of Antioch as a guest speaker and called them hypocrites; later, he took a whip to the money changers at the Temple. Now I'm not saying that you shouldn't go to church . . . it's just that you must go into church *with* God, not to find Him/Her. You see, God is in our homes and cars; He/She is everywhere we go and everywhere we are (including church, of course).

I'm reminded of the popular movie from several years ago called *Oh, God!* The most interesting parts of this film were when truisms were spouted, albeit tongue-in-cheek. One that hit me right between the eyes was when John Denver's character essentially asked God (played by George Burns) if Jesus Christ is the son of God. And God says something to the effect that yes he is—and so are you, and so is the man over there on the other side of the street, and so are all the others in this world. The point is, we all come from the same Creative Source.

Whatever you believe, be sure to come to know an all-loving Creator Who wants the best for you. We're all God's sons and daughters, and every single one of us has a spark of the Divine within. Never, ever, forget that.

✳ ✳ ✳ ✳ ✳ ✳

CONCLUSIONS

Thanks for coming along with me for another book. I hope it was as much a joy for you to read as it was for me to write. Now, instead of the same old Afterword, I'm going to end this book a little differently: with a list of the services we provide at the Society of Novus Spiritus, and a final discussion on dogmatic religion.

Novus Spiritus Services

Here's what we offer, along with an explanation of each service:

Prayer Groups

Numbering in the thousands, our prayer groups have been a tremendous success story. Here, a group of no more than 20 or 30 gather together to pore over Gnostic texts and philosophy. Such groups provide an atmosphere of fellowship for studying research transcripts and texts, and there's always a liaison with our church to field questions and provide answers. We try to keep the groups small so that study can be intensive and intimate, and this encourages participation by all.

The fees involved are very nominal—maybe costing a

few dollars or less per participant per month, depending on the group's size (fees are $20 per month for the entire group)—and they cover the expenses of paper and the publication of the study materials. Anyone can be a study-group member, or even start their own group.

For additional information, you can look on my Website, **www.sylvia.org**. You can also call (408) 379-7070, ext. 129; or e-mail **studygroup@novus.org**, and one of my ministers will be happy to help you.

Prayer/Crisis Line

The Society of Novus Spiritus also has a prayer/crisis line. This is utilized for those who call in with an illness or a problem (mental, physical, legal, economic, and so on), either for themselves or someone else, and we put their name on the prayer line. Then it begins to roll: The staff member who takes the name calls the study groups, and they in turn call others within the group so that it becomes hundreds of people praying at nine o'clock every night for all those on our list. Again, it doesn't matter if you know these people or even what their problem is . . . God does. We have hundreds of affidavits in our files from people who have been on the prayer line and either been healed or helped in some way.

You can contact our office to put yourself or someone else on the line, and there's no cost for this service. Please call (408) 379-7070, ext. 107; e-mail **office@sylvia.org**; or send a letter to 1700 Winchester Blvd., Suite 100, Campbell, CA 95008.

Letters

Finally, we at Novus Spiritus write letters to Mother God or to the universe (there is something not only powerful, but very cathartic, about writing down your needs). Then we burn or bury them and ask the Holy Spirit and angels to take our petition to Mother God. We also do this at our services, and the petitions we collect are burned by our ministers without anyone ever looking at them.

It's interesting to note that a few of our ministers who have collected the letters (again, without ever reading them), have dug holes in their garden and planted a bush, tree, or flower over them. One minister brought me a picture of the most magnificent rose bush that was planted over some of these petitions. It won a prize in the horticultural entries at the county fair: The roses, I kid you not, were as big as a baby's head!

A Final Word about Religion

To blame God for the suffering of humankind is completely erroneous. We can see how we mortal beings have created our own suffering thanks to our religious teachings, prejudices, morals, dogma, attitudes, intolerance . . . and the list can go on forever it seems.

So I'm going to end this book with an essay that was given to me by one of my followers who wishes to remain anonymous. Some of you might think it's a harsh commentary, but read it as more of a wake-up call so that we don't keep repeating the past. Read it with an open mind, for it applies to *all* religions, and because the trumpet of God will resound in your soul. (Note that it has been edited for clarity.)

Is Religion the Answer?

Religion is both the savior and bane of mankind. How many millions have been comforted by organized religion over the ages, and how many millions have been killed, tortured, raped, and plundered over these same ages? How many religions have not been persecuted? The answer is none. *All* religions have been persecuted at some point in their histories, and that continues to this day. In this modern "civilization," we still have not learned to love and tolerate one another. We have all the problems of economy, racism, ethnic purging, discrimination, hunger, poverty, politics, power, greed, terrorism, and on and on . . . seemingly endless it goes. Isn't this world wonderful? No wonder we're all depressed and tired—we hear about and experience these problems every day. It has got to stop, or the generations that follow us will have nothing.

We must start with organized religion, for it's both part of the problem and the key to the salvation of the world. The major religions of the world have got to band together and not only preach but practice religious tolerance.

Islam, the fastest-growing religion in the world today, has got to go back to its roots of religious tolerance (it is one of the most tolerant of religions) and oust the extremists who practice terrorism in the name of a holy Jihad (holy war) on the "infidels" of other religions or countries. Most of the message from Mohammed was Christlike, teaching love and tolerance for others . . . his teachings have been warped by extremists and conservative clerics who lust for power and greed at any cost of human life. Most Muslims are very devout and loving people who treat others with respect and kindness; but extremists are grabbing the headlines and perpetuating their wars against Israel, India, Europe, and the United States by playing on the emotions of the followers of Islam in their self-proclaimed "holy war."

Peace will never be obtained through terrorism, for it is the method of despicable evil. Peace can only be obtained through tolerance and negotiation in which both sides bend and compromise. Gone is the day when military might could conquer and bring a forced peace—the world will not stand for any country conquering and taking over another (the United States included). Yes, we still have places such as Iraq and Afghanistan that were subdued by military might, but the outrage of the world was heard, and these countries are being given back to the people that inhabit them. The world of Islam must go back to its messenger and practice what he brought forth in love and tolerance to climb that mountain of self.

Christianity also has some major problems that it must face. The Catholic Church has many internal problems that hurt others, and it's on the wane because it's slow to change and make compromises. It has lost the respect of many for its many internal scandals and failure to acknowledge its mistakes both in the past and present. It has trapped itself in its own unbendable traditions and become stagnant, and certainly makes less of an impact on the world today. It must make wholesale changes or it will go down, as so many inflexible dynasties have, and not be the powerful voice it once was.

The Protestant movement is also becoming more inflexible and conservative, with its right-wing politics creating myriad problems in the forms of bigotry, intolerance, and its propensity to try to gain power in the political arena. What's the old adage—religion and politics don't mix well? Christianity is one of the least tolerant toward other religions, which makes the task of bonding with other worldwide religions, in order to accomplish an overall good for the world, seem near to impossible, but it must be done.

Christianity today has become warped in many areas, namely that of preaching and practicing the worship of an all-loving and merciful God. Many churches concentrate more on the "hellfire and brimstone" approach to battling evil, invoking the fear of God and His wrath on those who "sin," or constantly using the Bible to rule their congregations by fear. It seems like a complete contradiction to me, as Christ always preached about an all-loving and merciful God. Some of these so-called Christian churches use the Bible so much that they ought to be named "Bible worshipers" instead of "worshipers of Christ."

If Christ was to come down to the world today, I doubt he'd proclaim himself a Christian. Christianity needs to practice more religious tolerance, get out of the political arena, and really put forth the concept of an all-loving and merciful God—rather than a wrathful, vengeful God Who has all of the imperfect emotions of mankind. In order for Christianity to take its place in saving this world, they have got to leave their hidden agendas of politics and getting wealthy behind and put forth the agenda of Christ. They have got to climb that mountain of ego that has been built up with their wealth and power and get down to helping others in the way that Christ would have wanted . . . no matter what their ethnic, racial, religious, or sexual background may be.

If you want people to be a part of your religion, do it with the truth and the love of God, not with your own self-righteous agendas. Concentrate more on the joy, truth, and love of God, not your own human-made truth . . . for you should at least be able to recognize that you may be wrong. Christianity has always been ruled by fear and money: the fear of being wrong and the money to build more churches (to get even more money). Its bloody history and its intolerance toward other faiths and beliefs proves this to be true. The Christian motto seems to be: *If you're threatened in your faith, for God's sake don't tolerate the right of others to believe otherwise. Instead, just destroy them, whether it be from the pulpit, in the political arena, with propaganda, or the sword.*

I know I'm on a soapbox, and I know I'm being tough and harsh in my criticism of some of these major religions, but damn it, someone has got to speak up. The religions of this world have to band together to help the planet, not tear it apart and asunder with their own agendas. I know that there are millions out there who aren't being helped by the faith they're now following, and I know that there are millions out there who have left their faith because it didn't give them the truth and comfort they were seeking. It's such a tragedy that the major religions of this world have messed up the simple act of worshiping God. God created us all in our many different colors and ethnic backgrounds, and He even sent messengers to help us find the way to His all-loving, merciful, and perfect Self. We turn around and disregard or warp all that and make war and commit atrocities on each other. It is the tragedy of tragedies.

We live in a time of exciting spiritual awareness and freedom of thought, so don't waste it in a box of dogma. As the poem goes: "God's in His heaven [and with you] / And all's right with the world" . . . if it isn't, make it all right in *your* world and the world around you.

God love you, I do,
Sylvia

* * * * * *

ABOUT THE AUTHOR

Sylvia Browne is the #1 *New York Times* best-selling author and world-famous psychic medium who appears regularly on the *Montel Williams Show* and *Larry King Live,* as well as making countless other media and public appearances. With her down-to-earth personality and great sense of humor, Sylvia thrills audiences on her lecture tours—and she's still found the time to write a number of immensely popular books (she has a master's degree in English literature). Sylvia lives in California and plans to write as long as she can.

Please contact Sylvia at: **www.sylvia.org**, or call **(408) 379-7070** for further information about her work.

✻ ✻ ✻ ✻ ✻ ✻

Hay House Titles of Related Interest

The Alchemist's Handbook, by John Randolph Price

Diary of a Psychic, by Sonia Choquette

The Disappearance of the Universe, by Gary R. Renard

Goddesses & Angels, by Doreen Virtue, Ph.D.

I Want to See Jesus in a New Light, by Ron Roth, Ph.D.

The New Golden Rules, by Dharma Singh Khalsa, M.D.

Practical Praying, by John Edward

Secrets of the Lost Mode of Prayer, by Gregg Braden

7 Paths to God, by Joan Z. Borysenko, Ph.D.

The Unbelievable Truth, by Gordon Smith

All of the above are available at your
local bookstore, or may be ordered by visiting:

Hay House USA: **www.hayhouse.com**
Hay House Australia: **www.hayhouse.com.au**
Hay House UK: **www.hayhouse.co.uk**
Hay House South Africa: **orders@psdprom.co.za**

✳ ✳ ✳

NOTES

NOTES

NOTES

NOTES

NOTES

NOTES

NOTES

NOTES

NOTES

NOTES